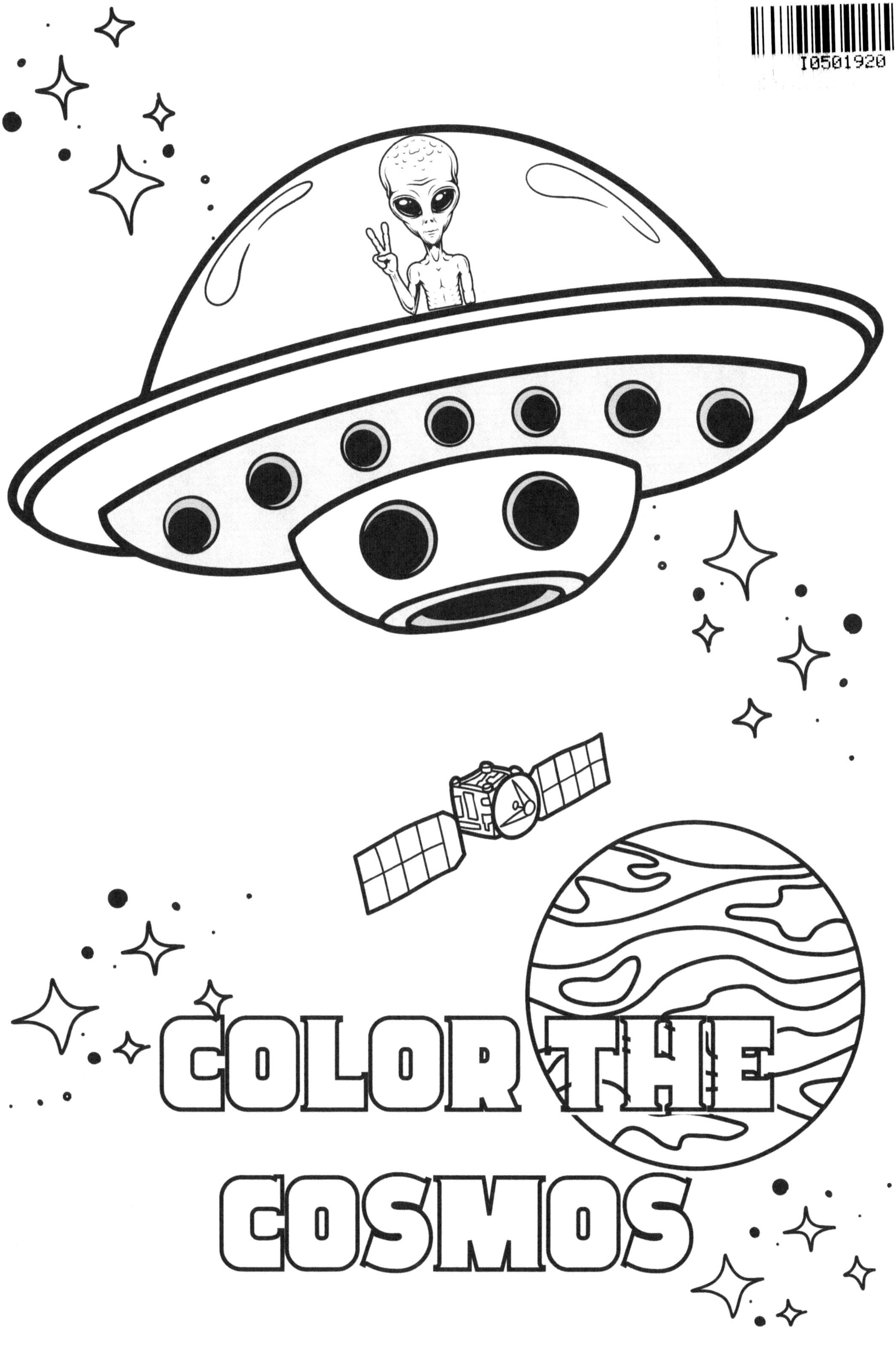

COLOR THE COSMOS

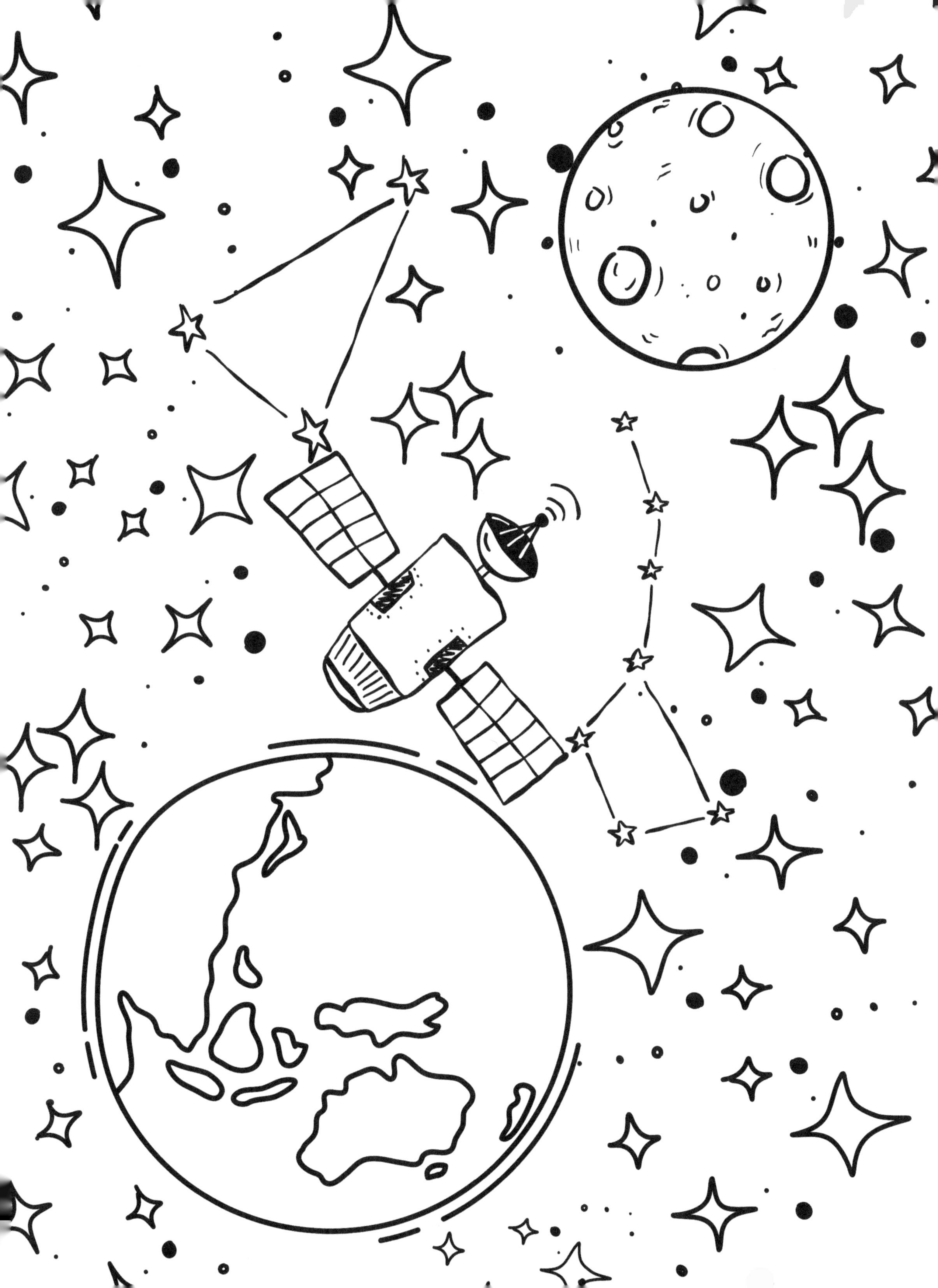

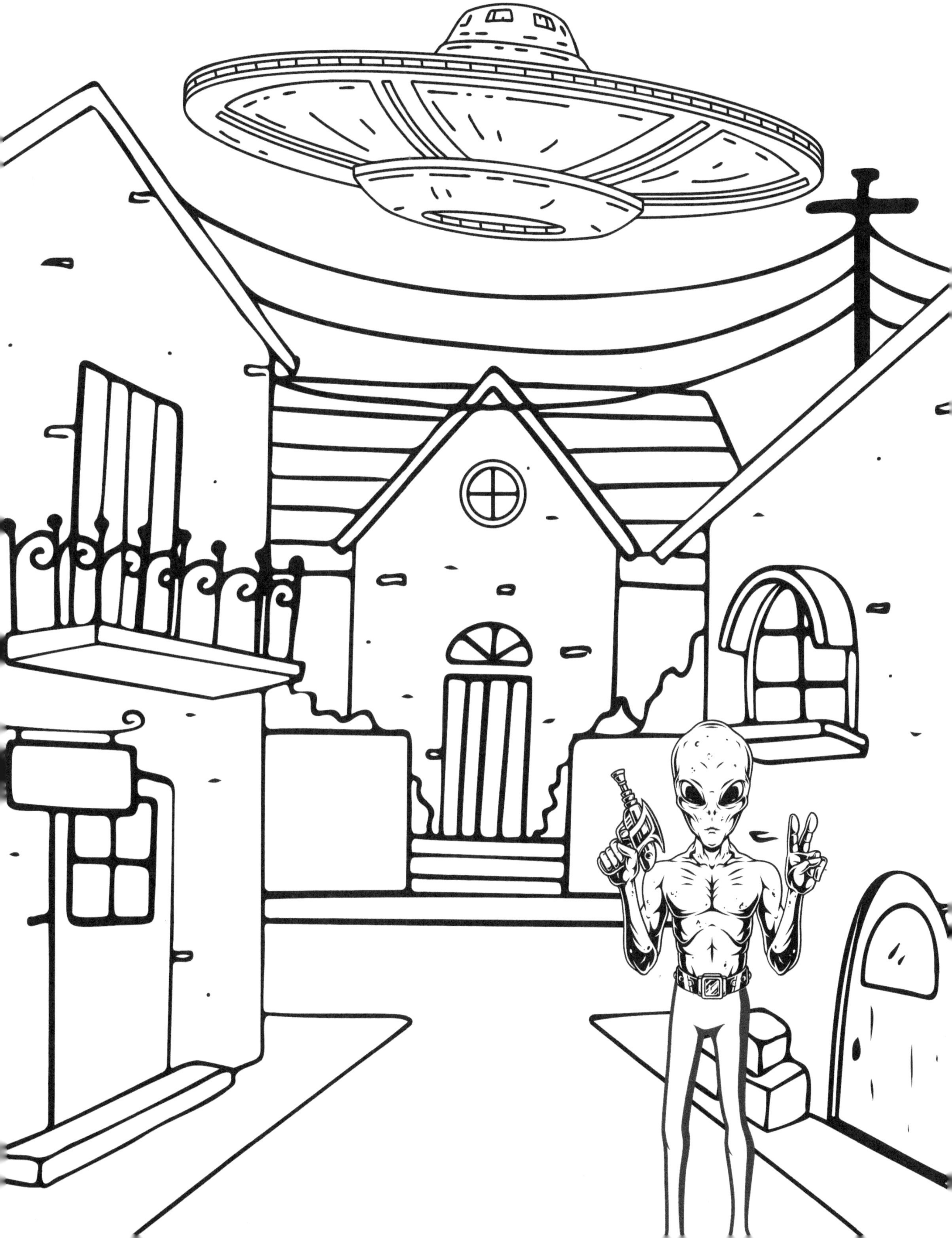

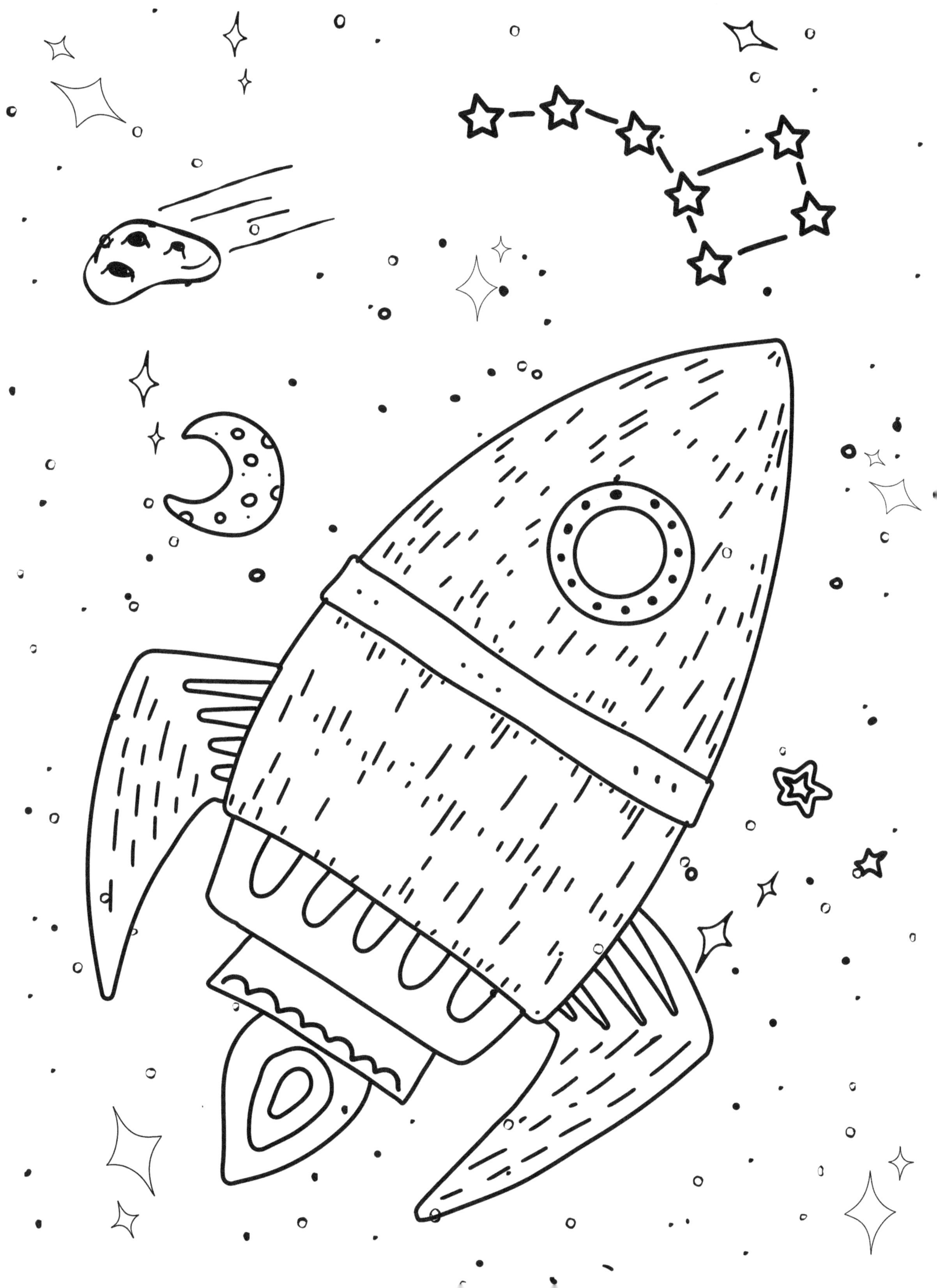

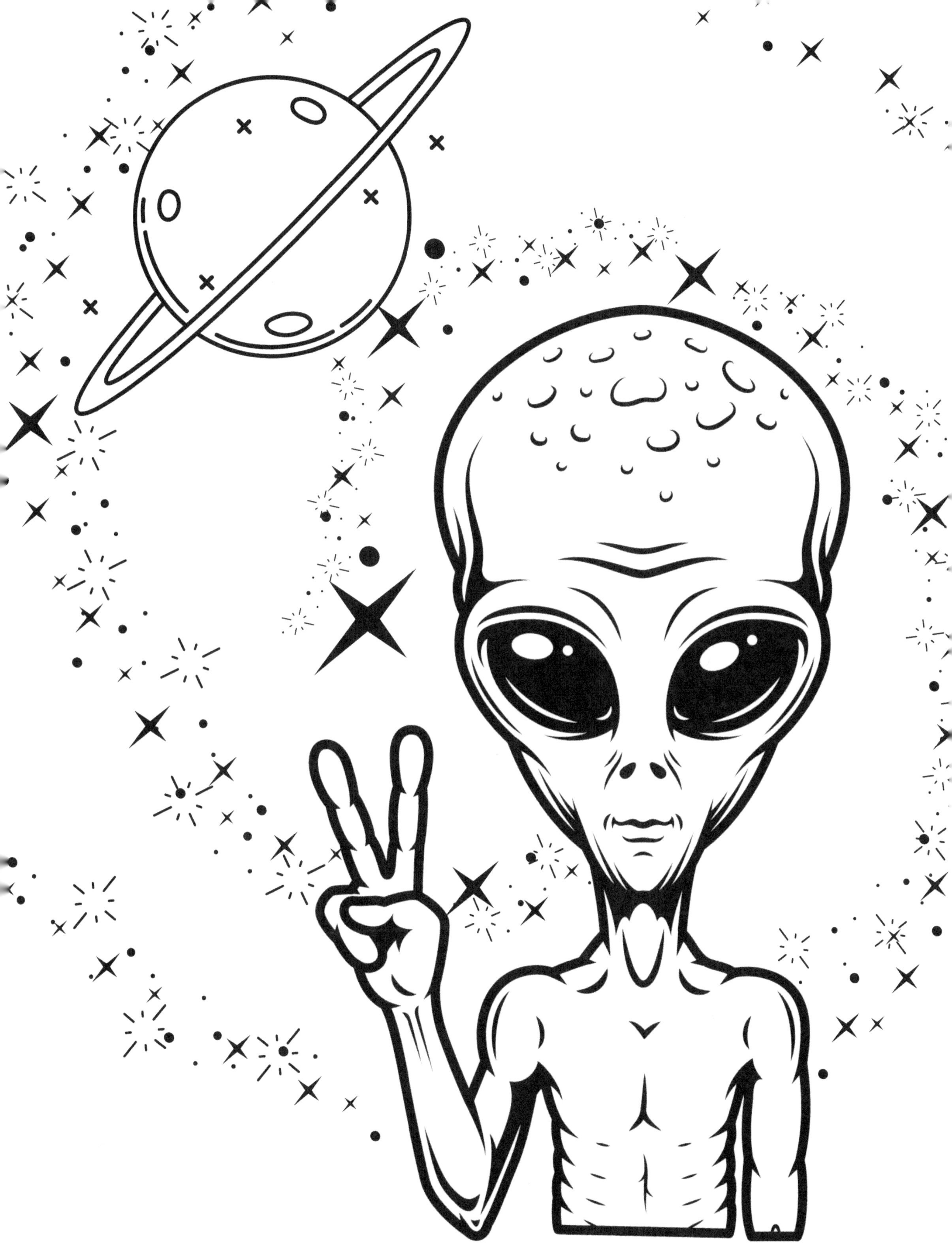

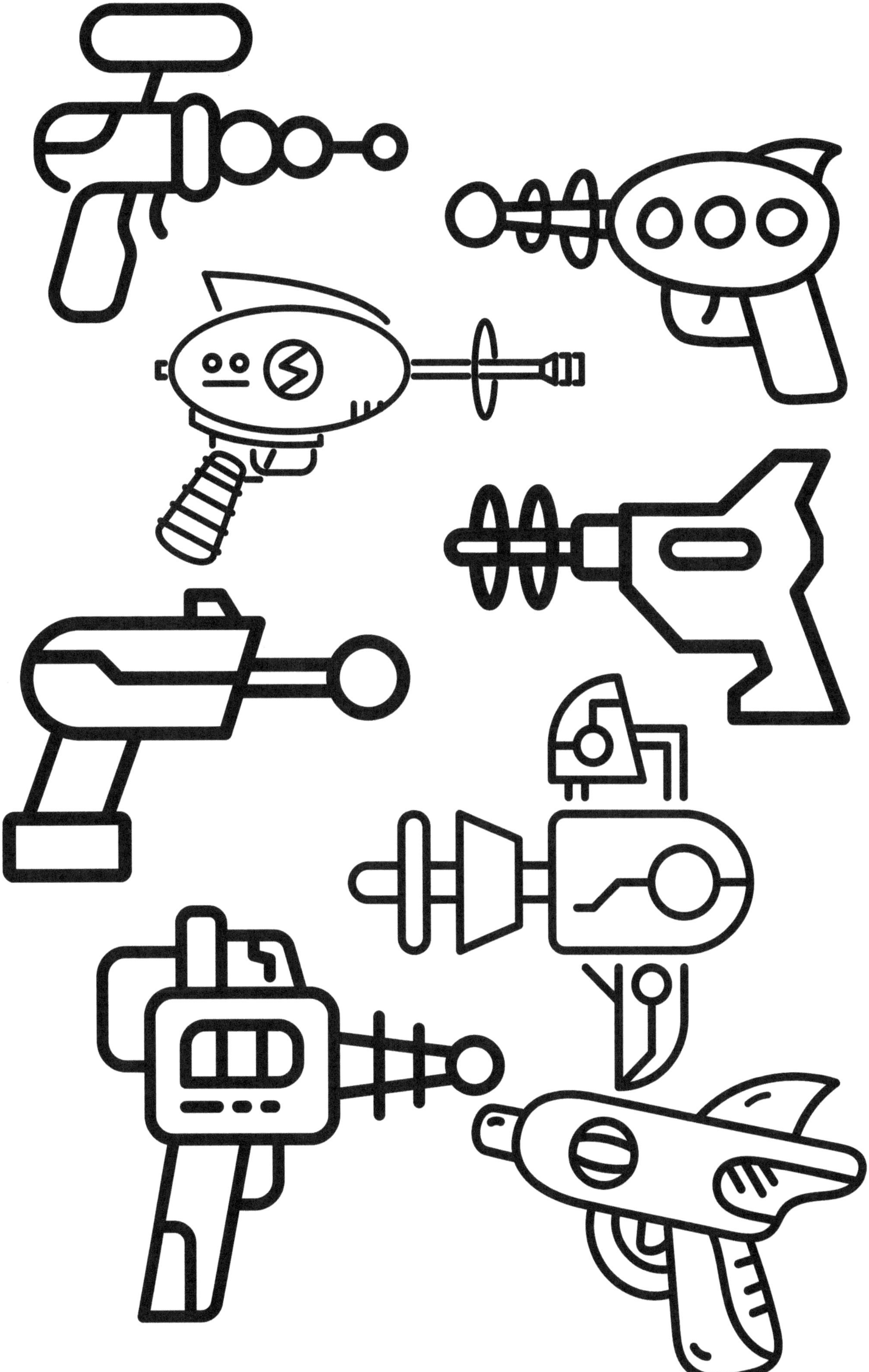

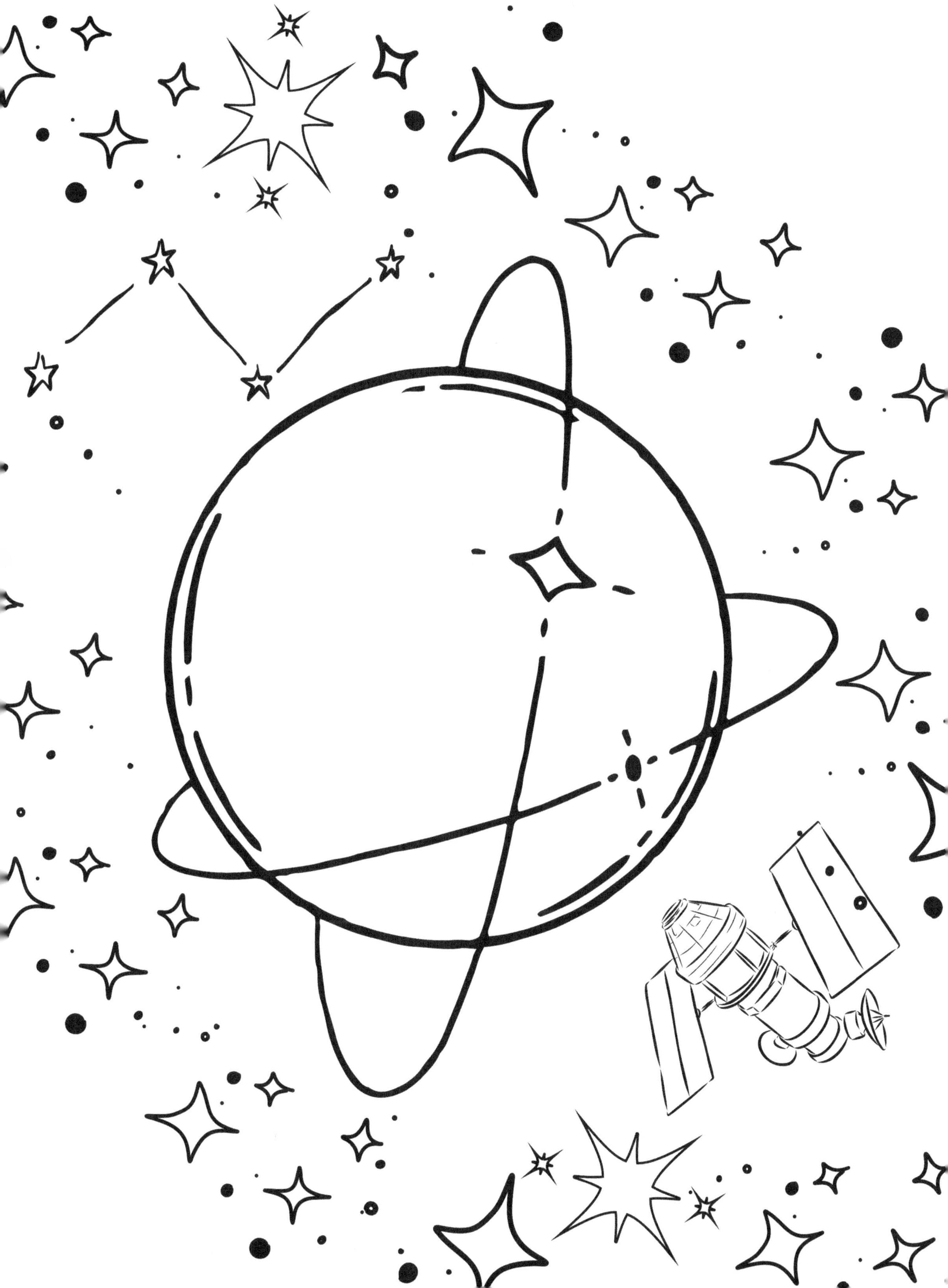

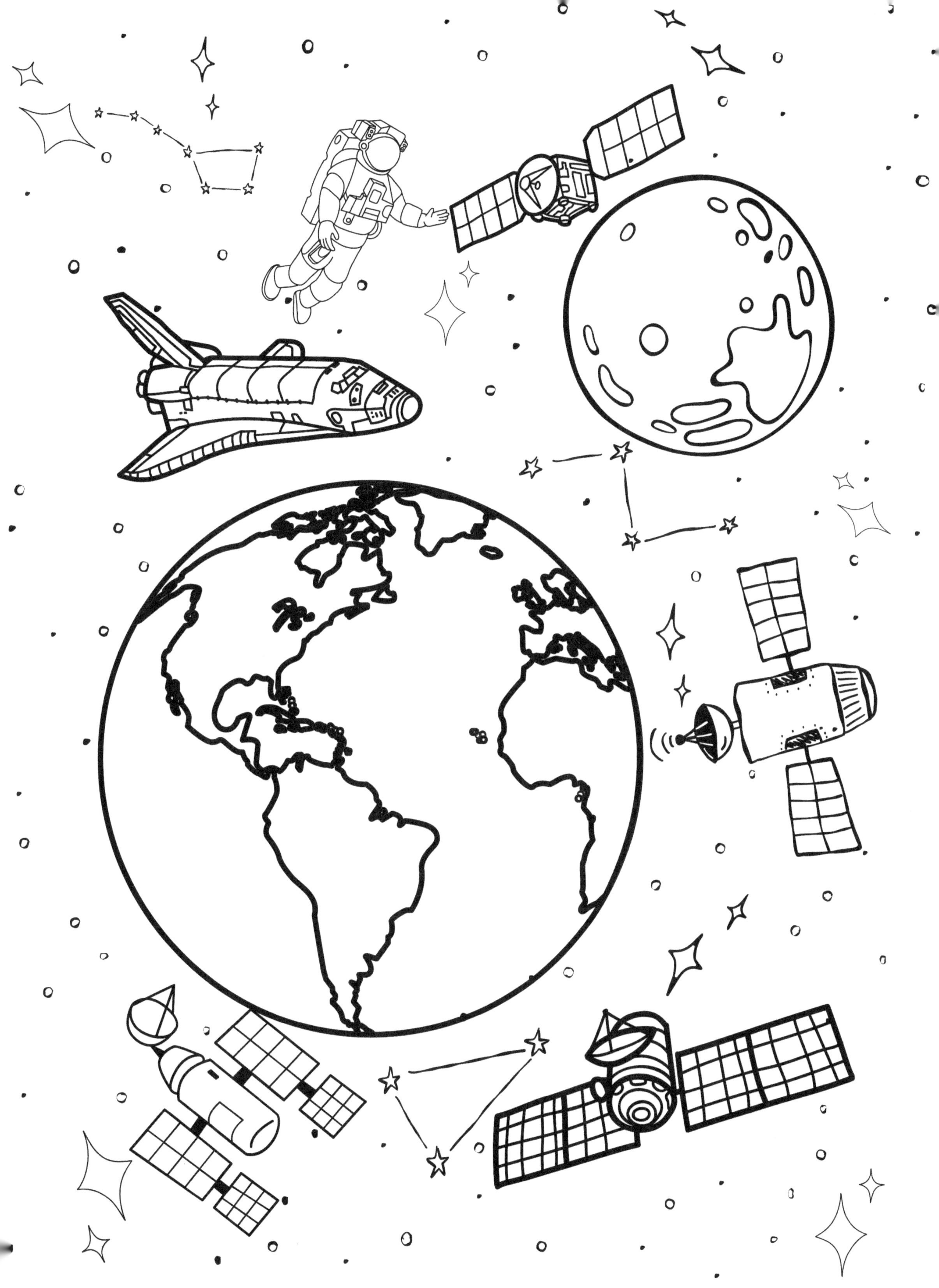

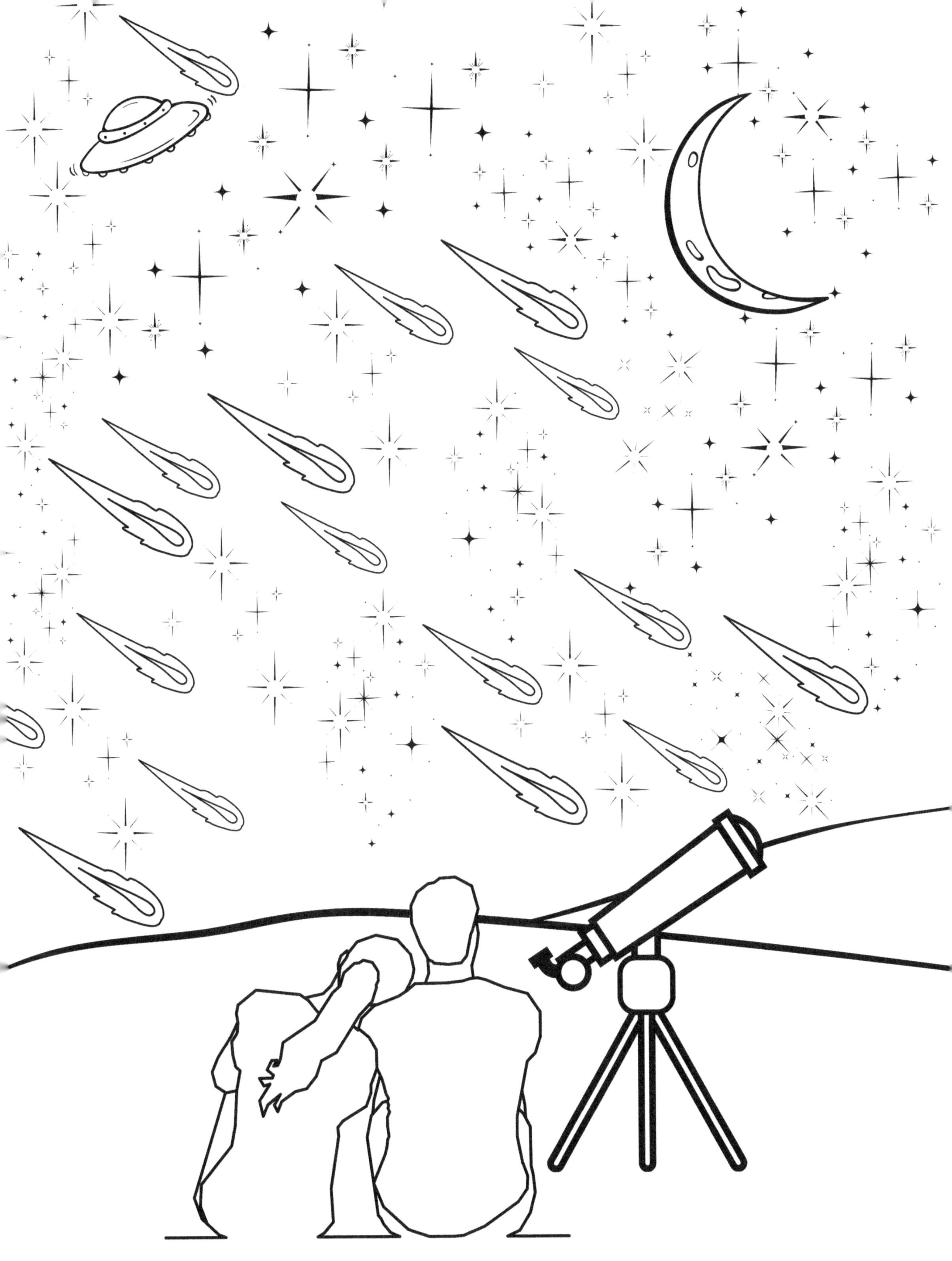

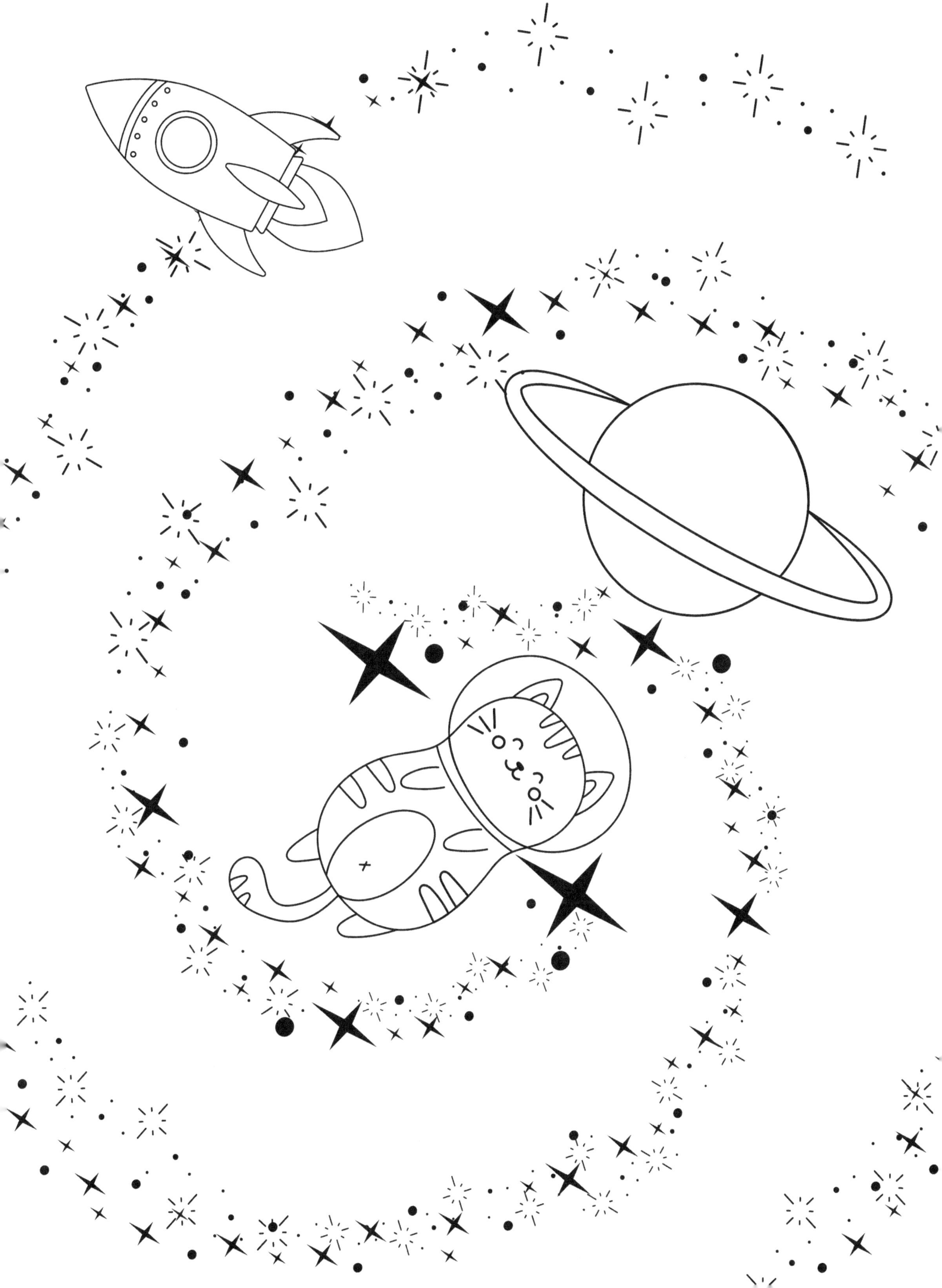

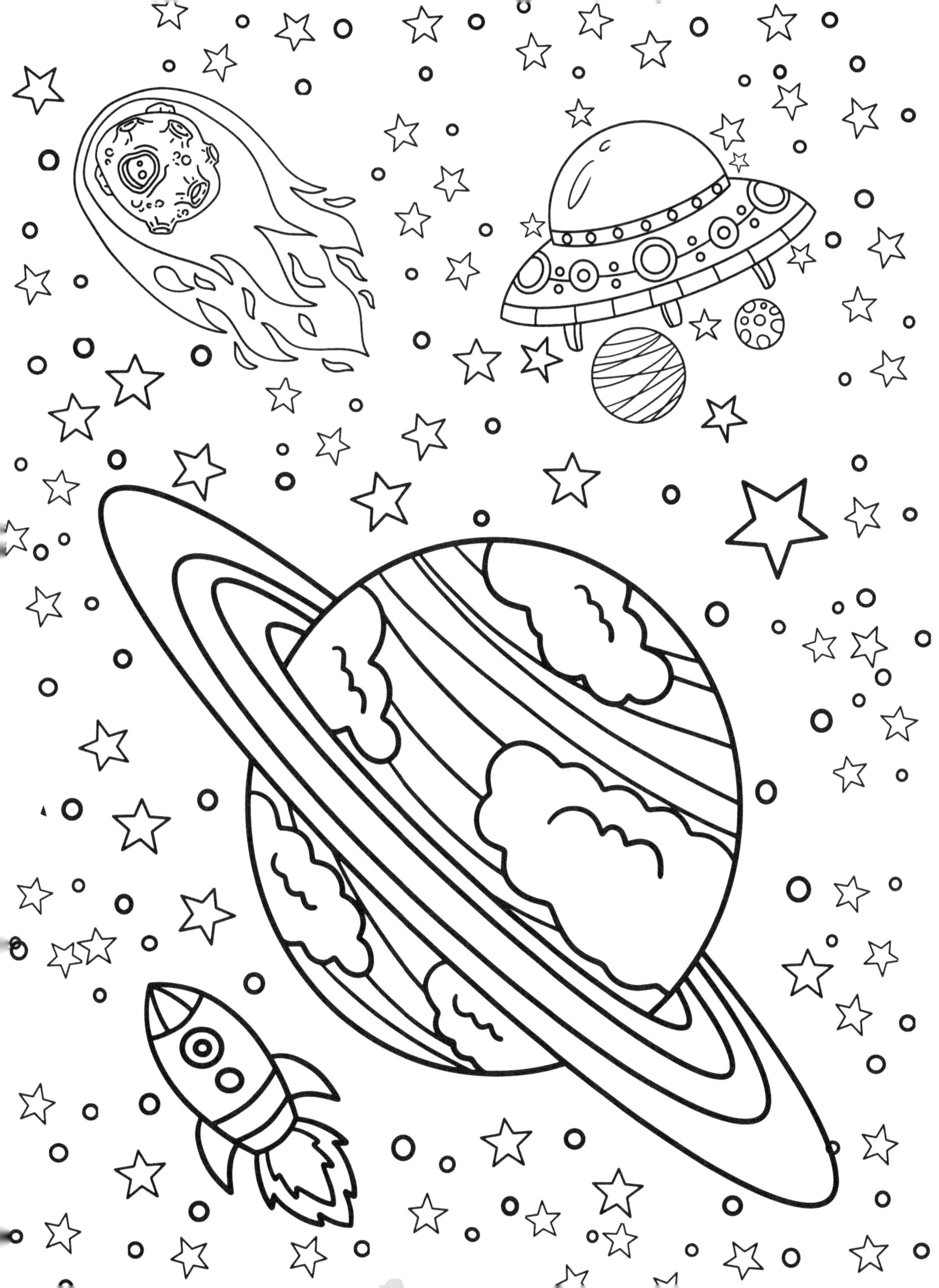

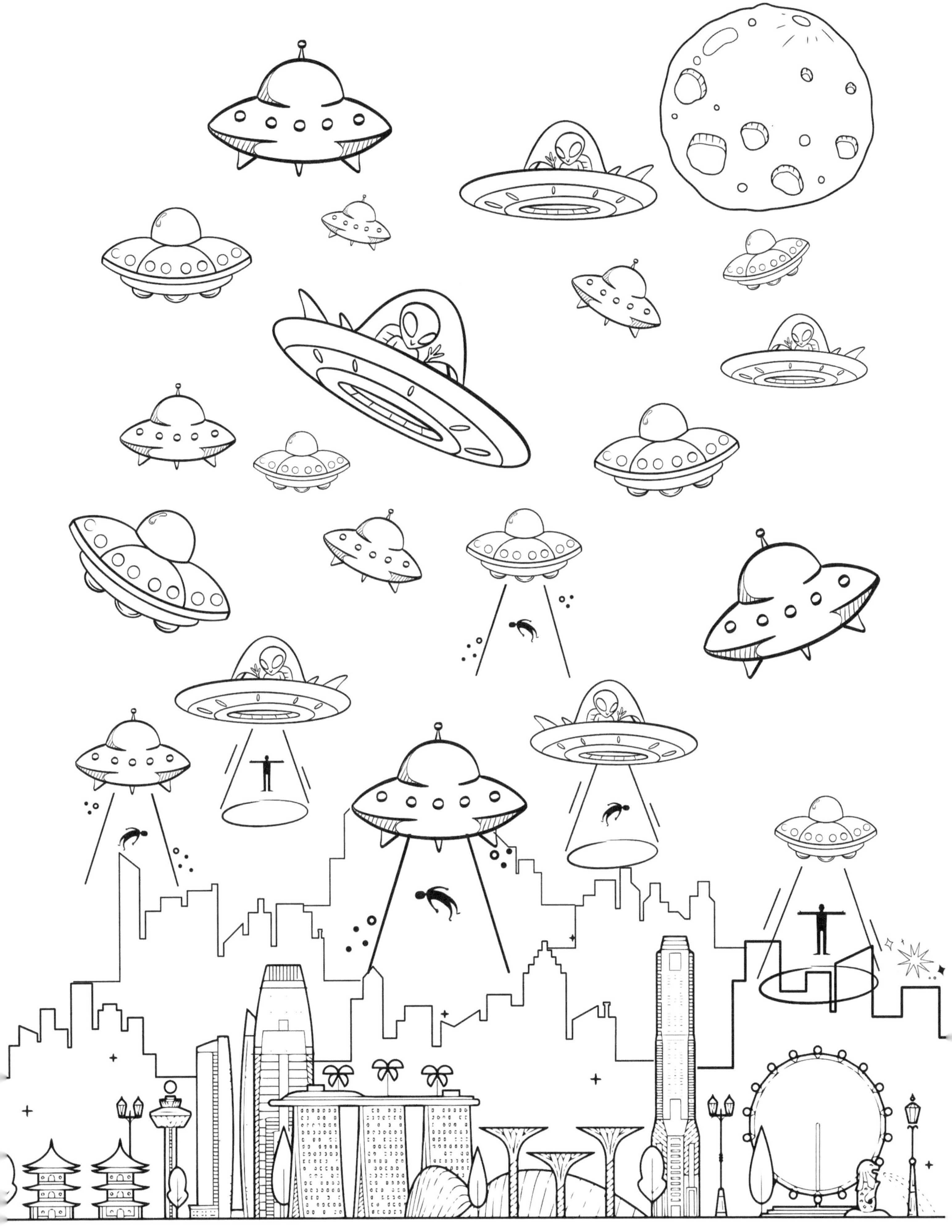

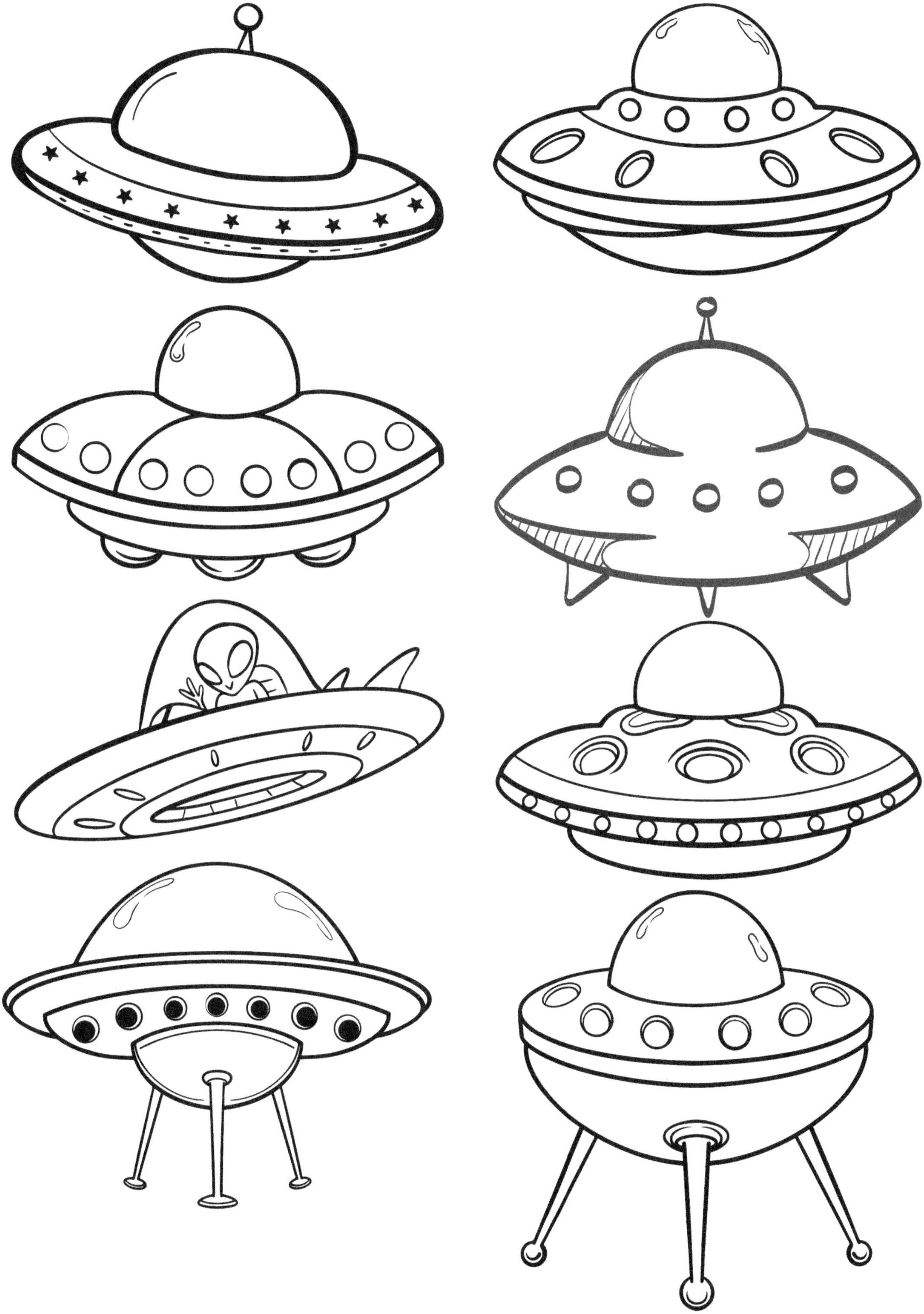

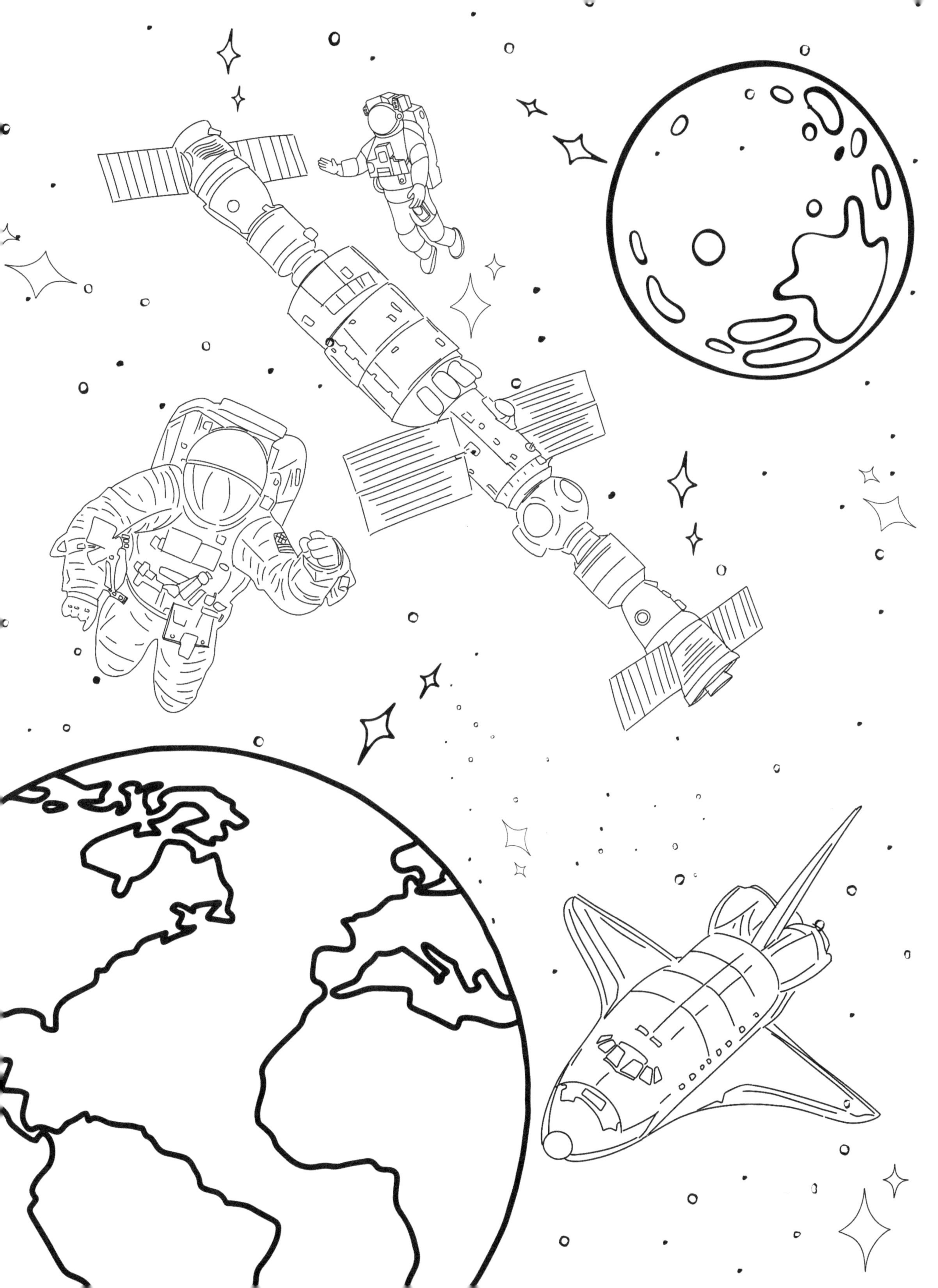

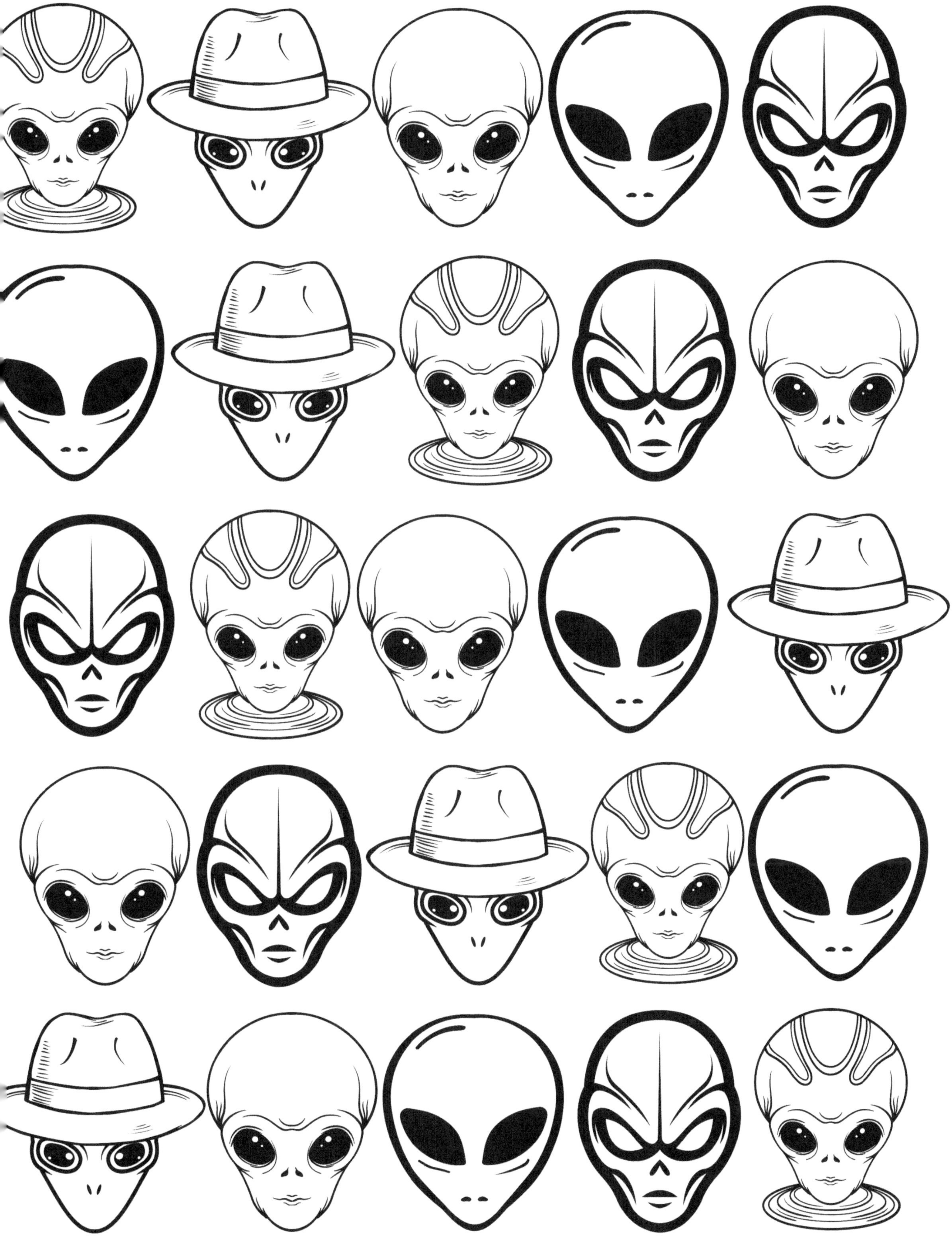

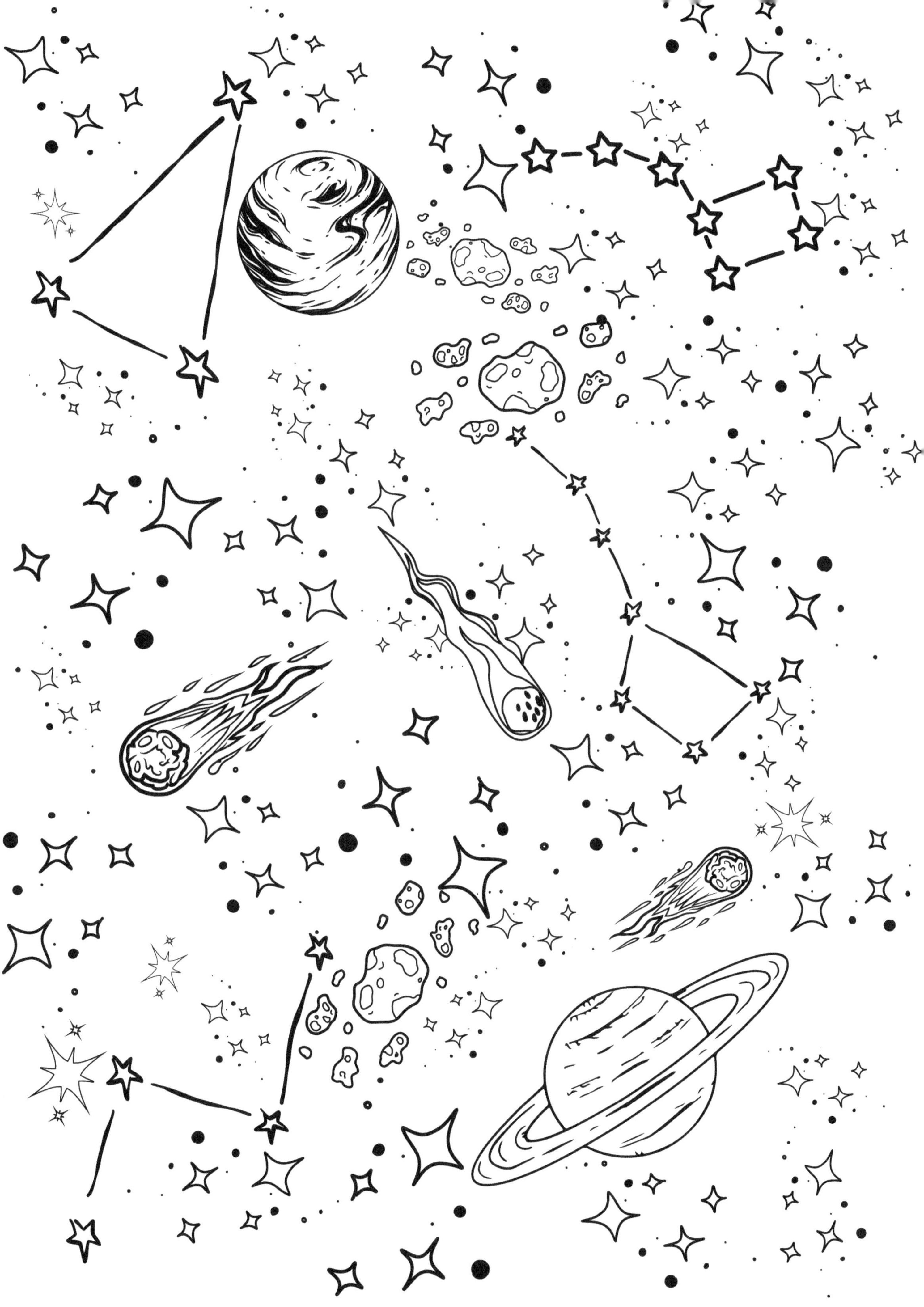

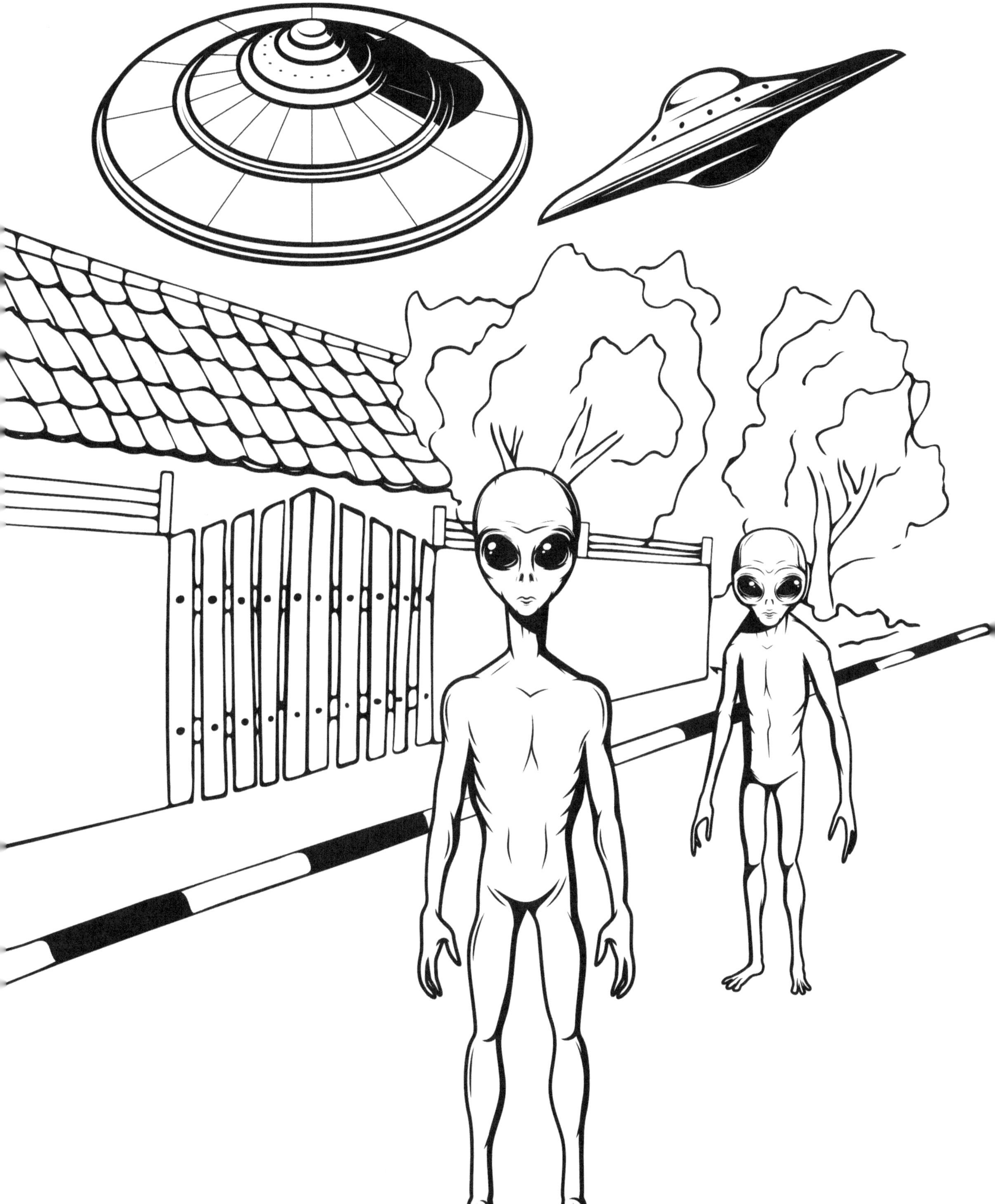

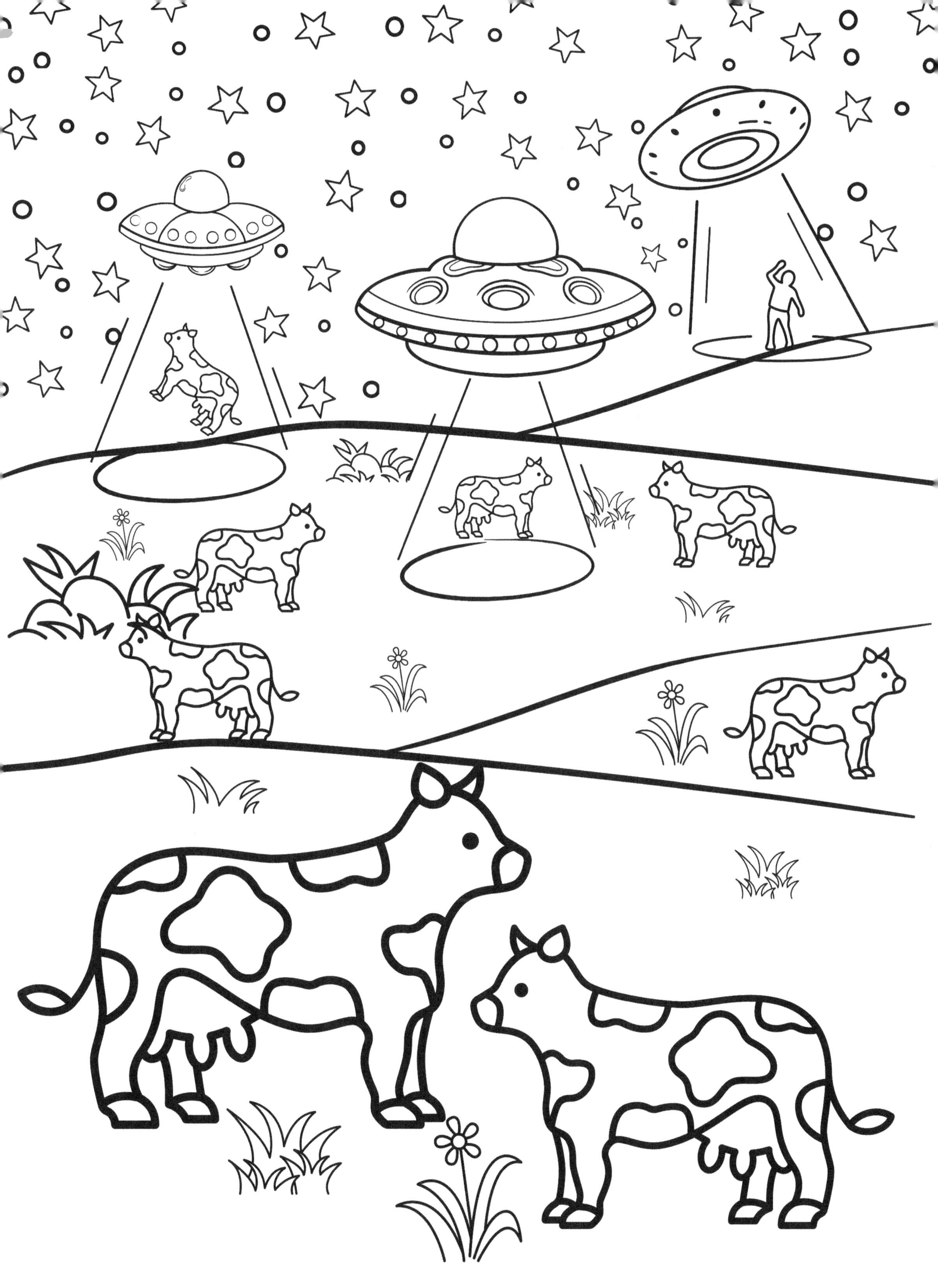

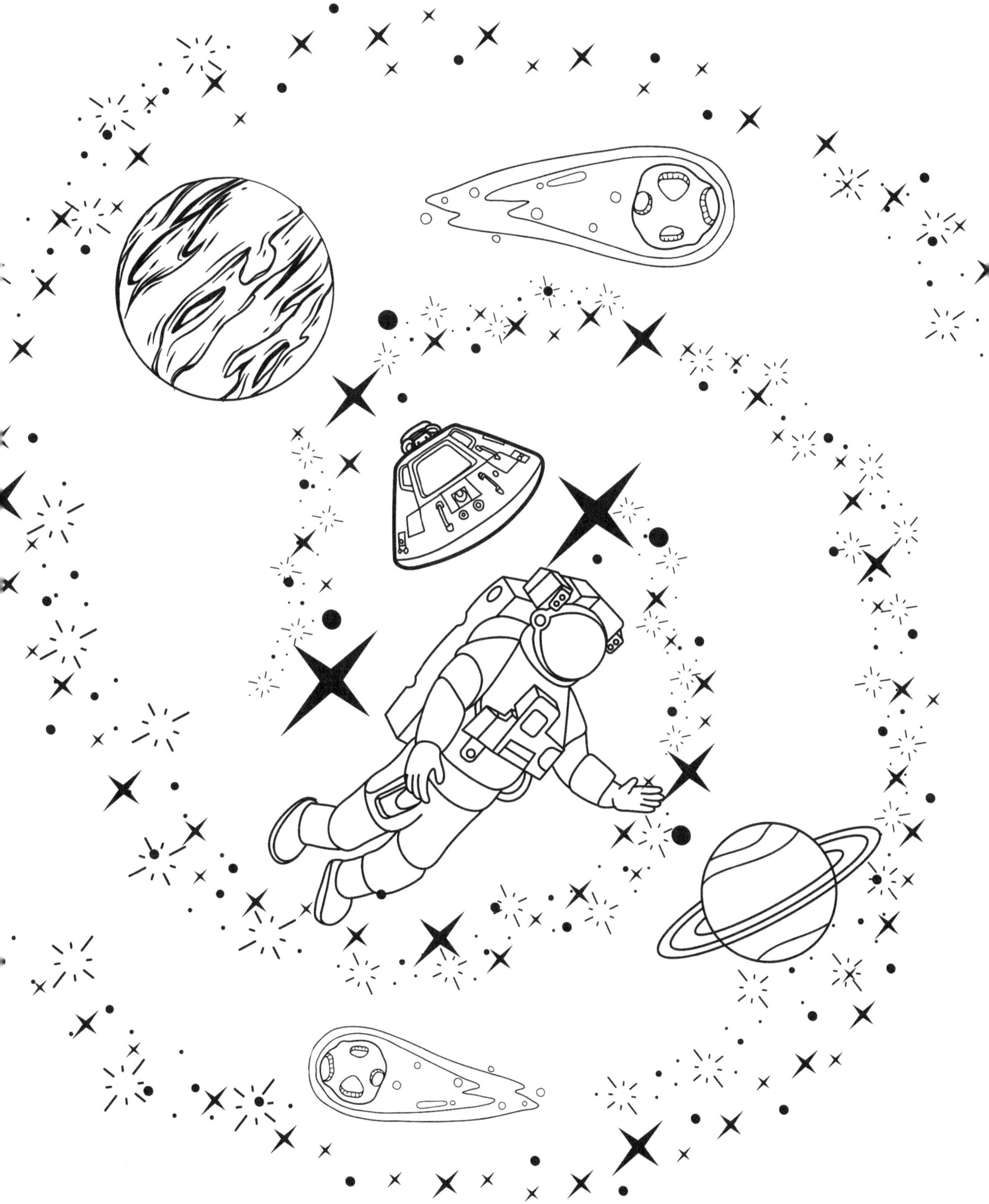

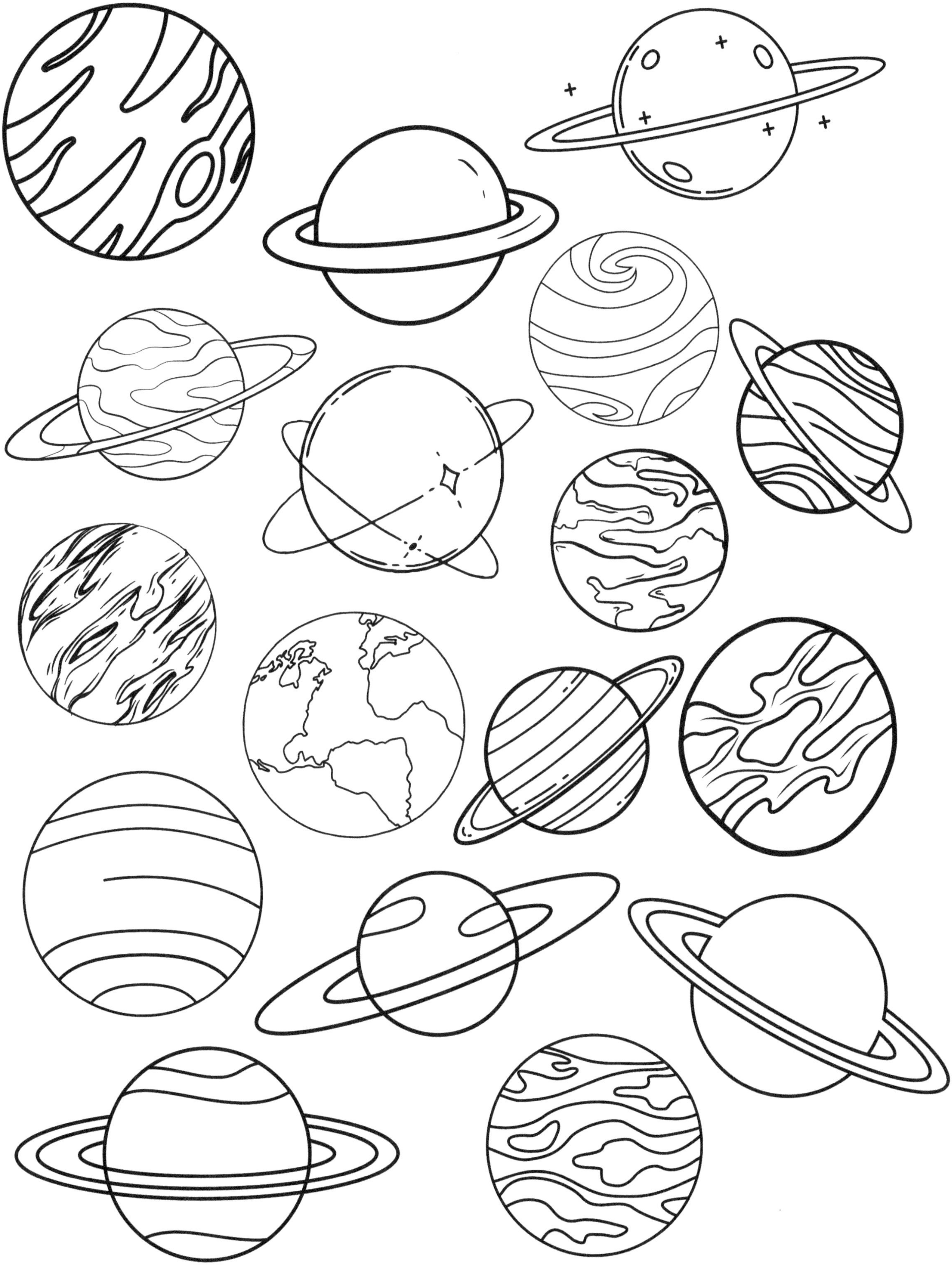

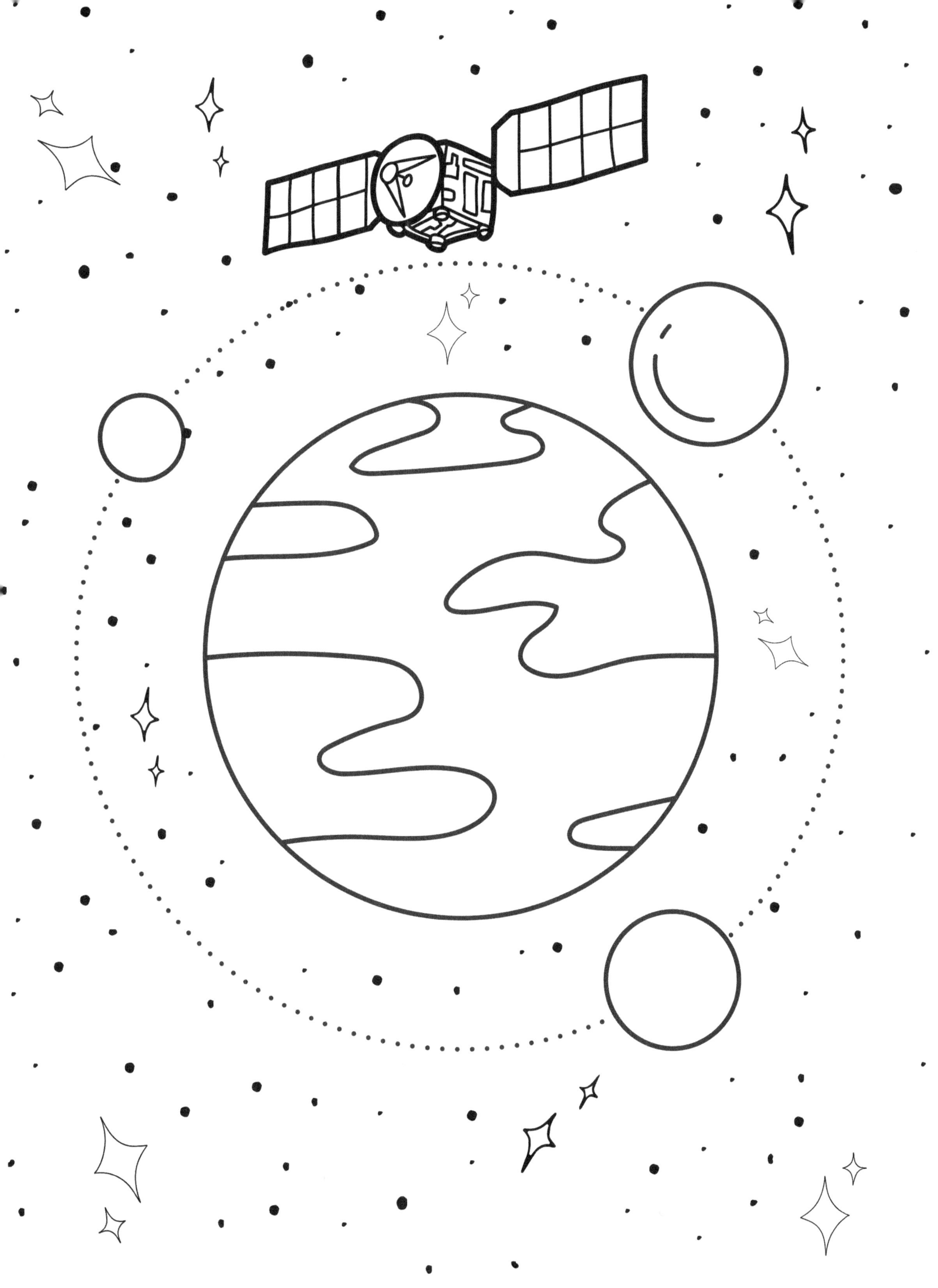

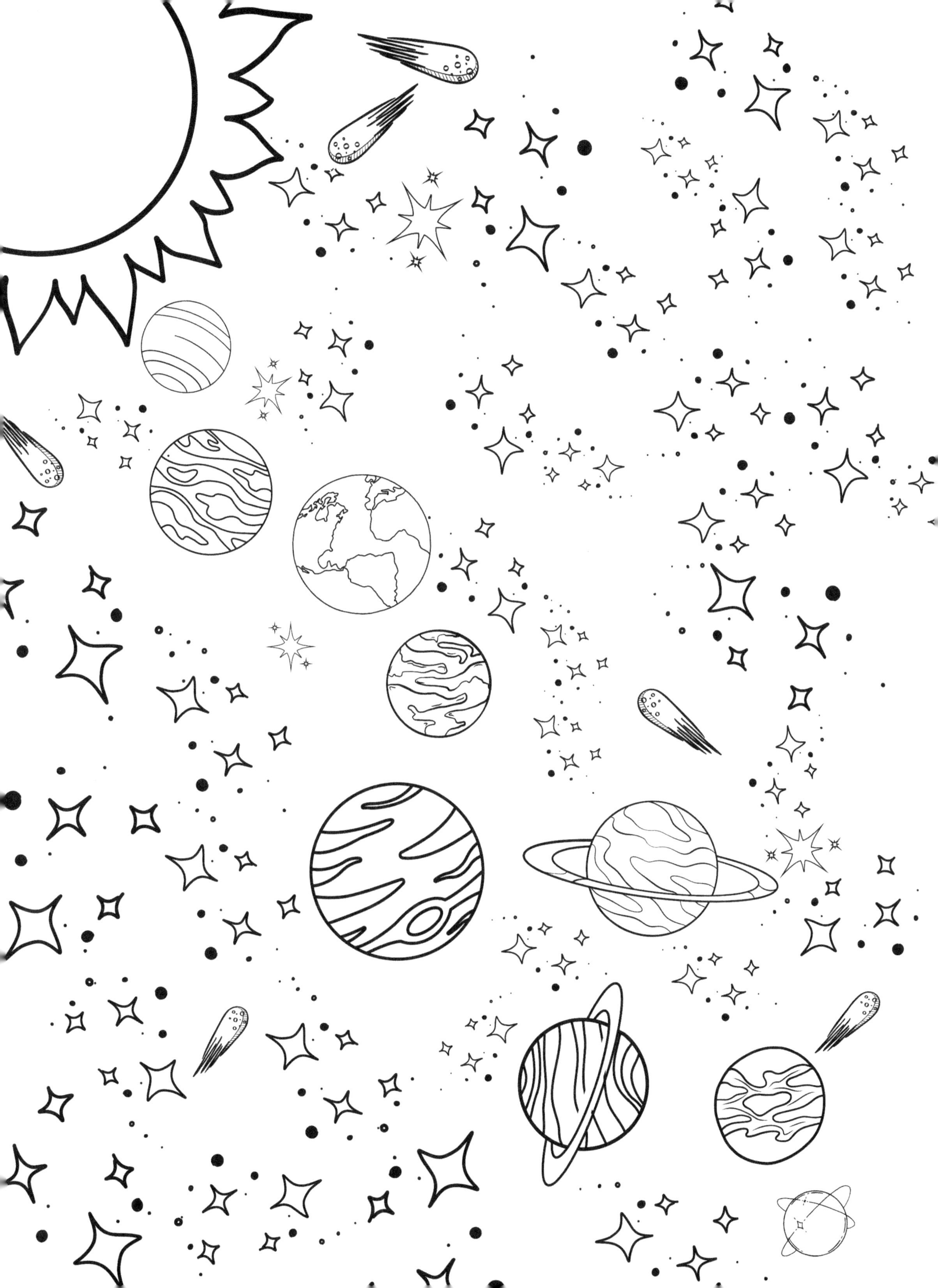

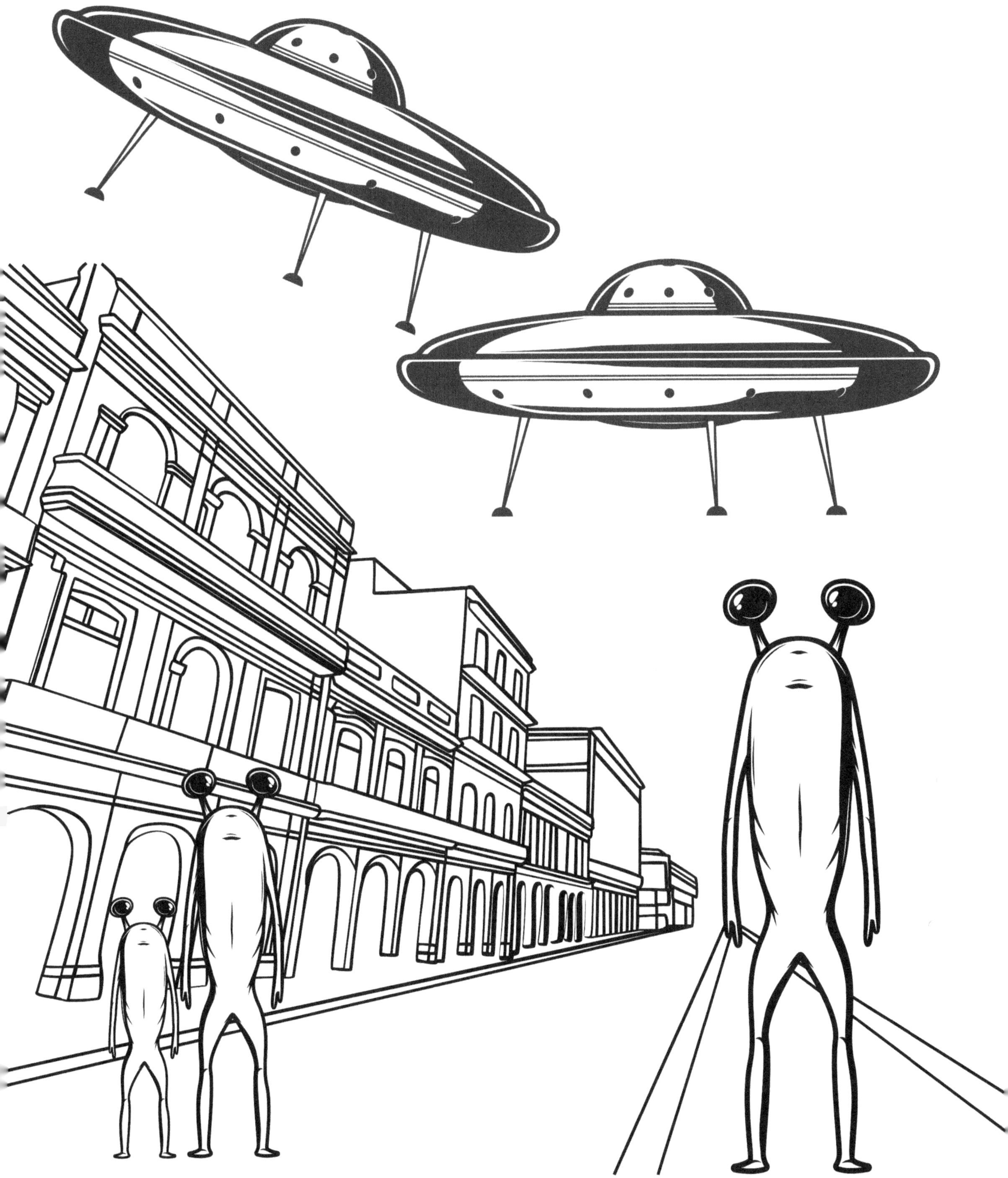

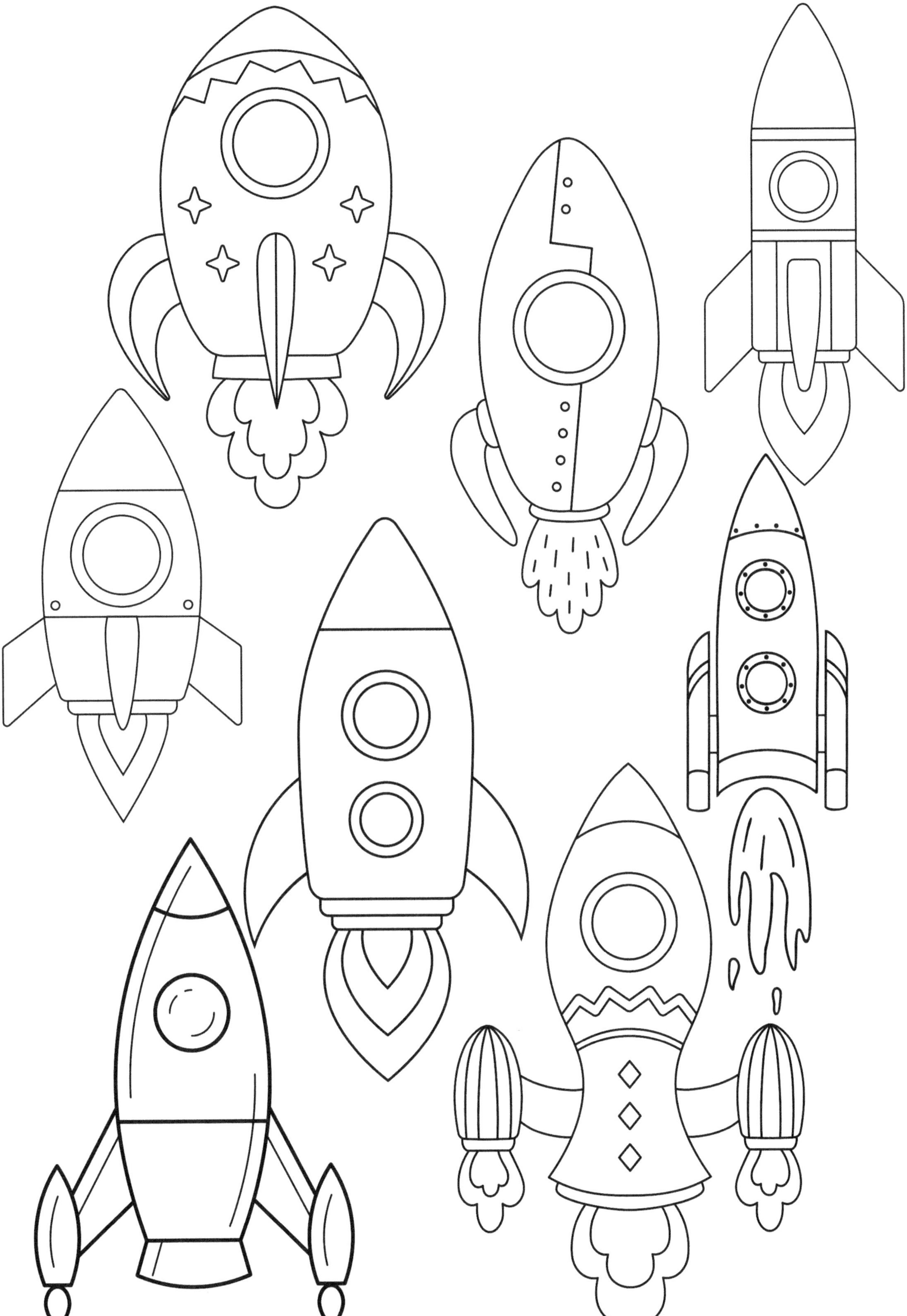

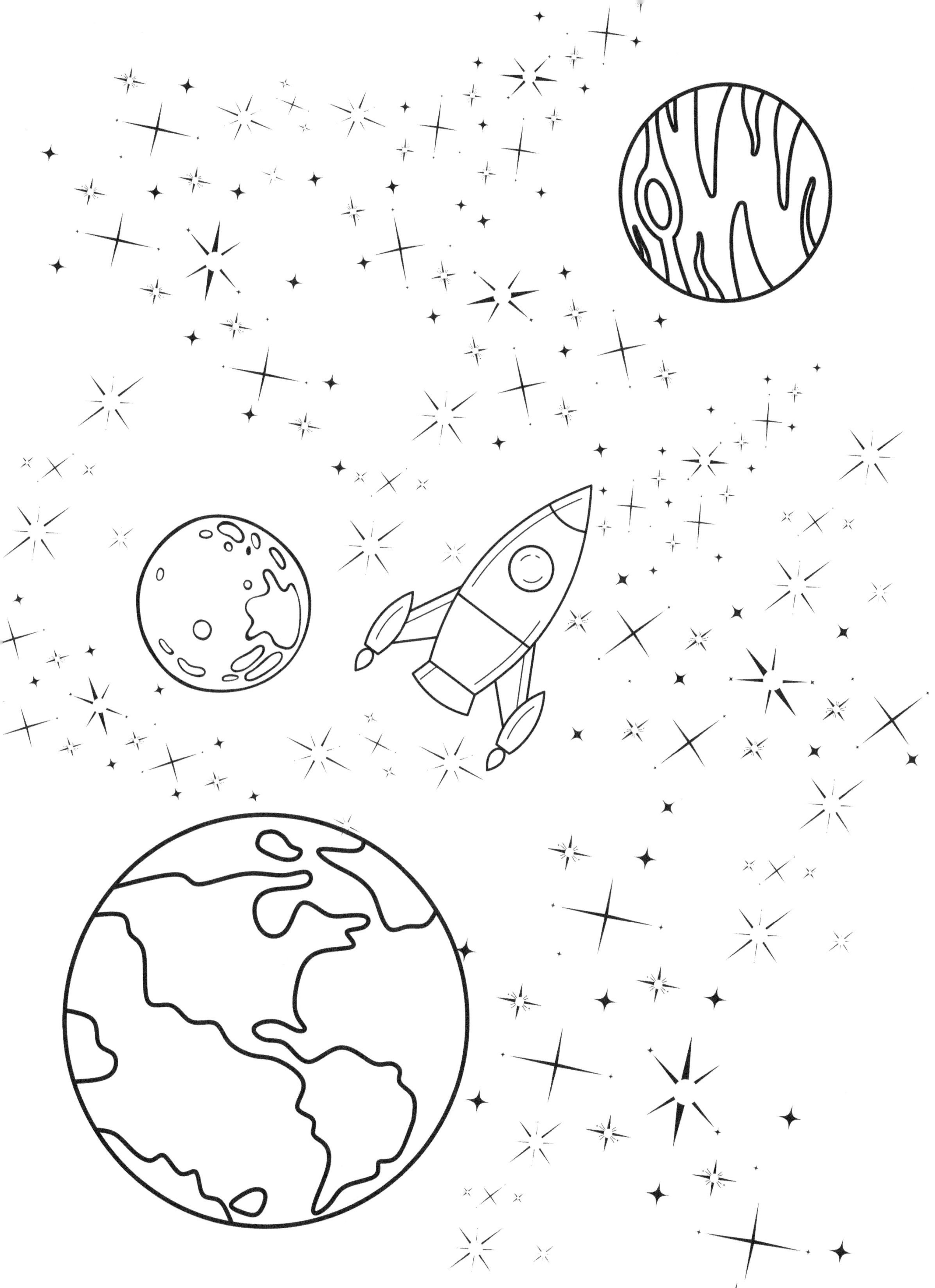

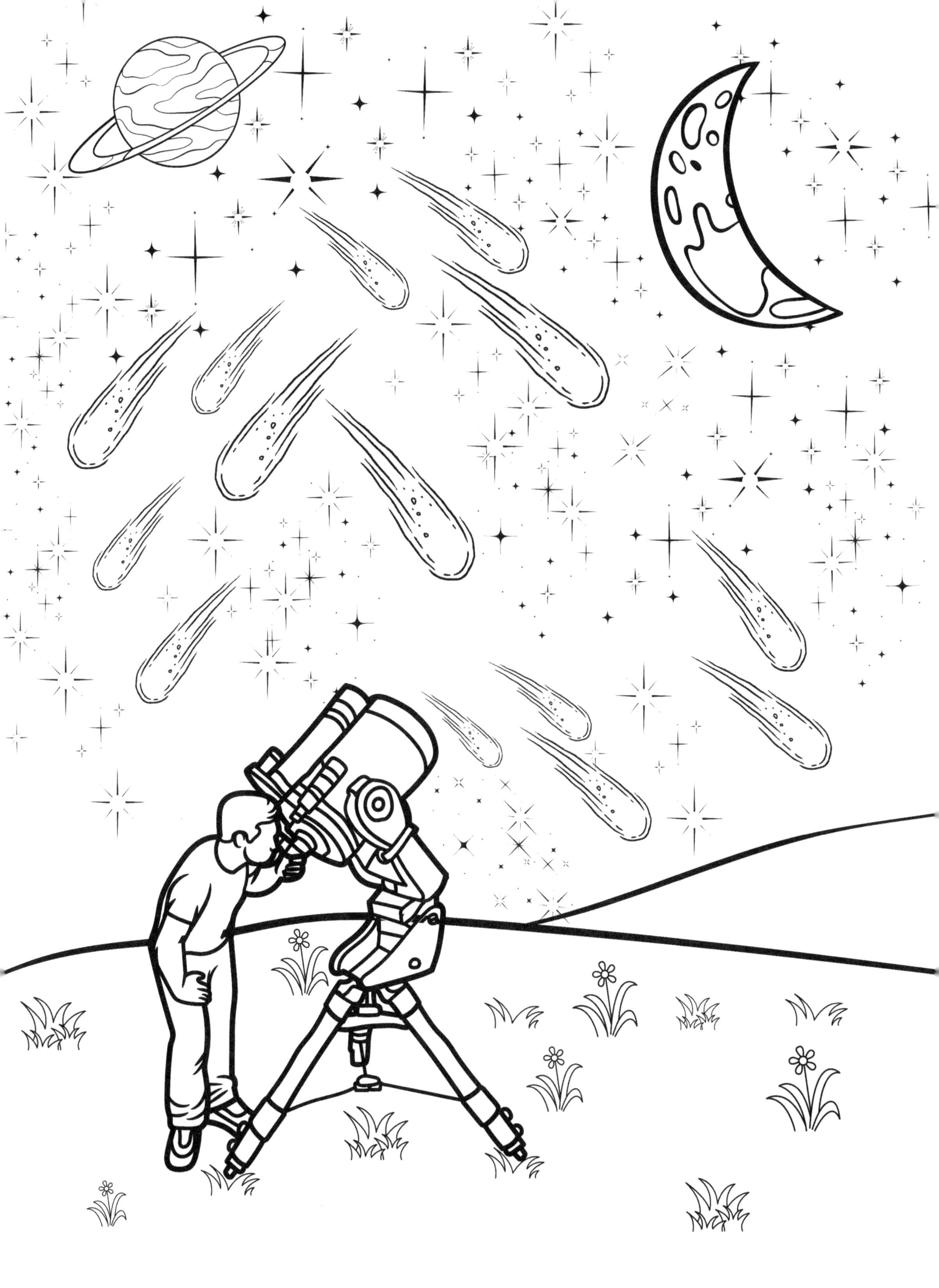

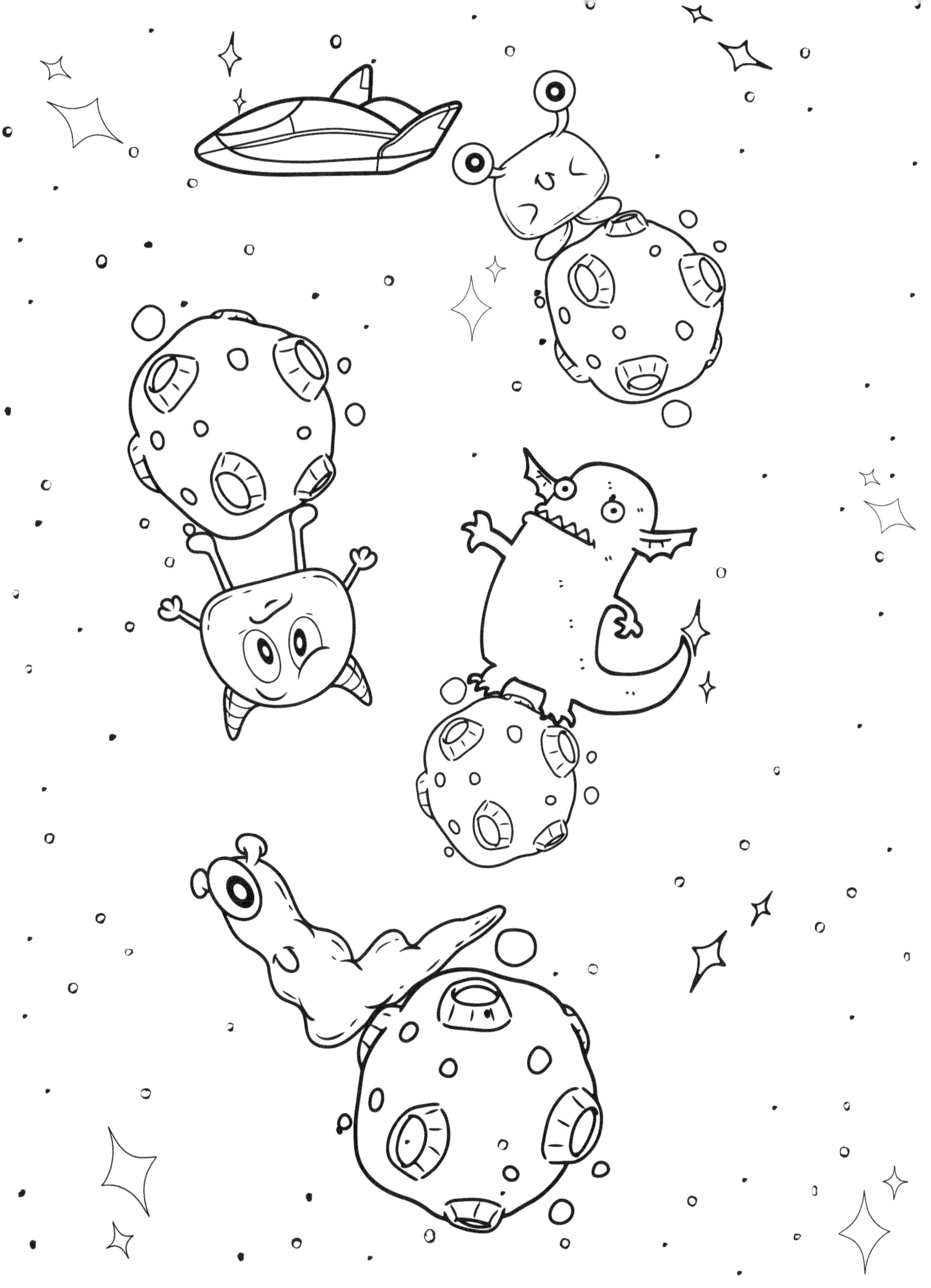

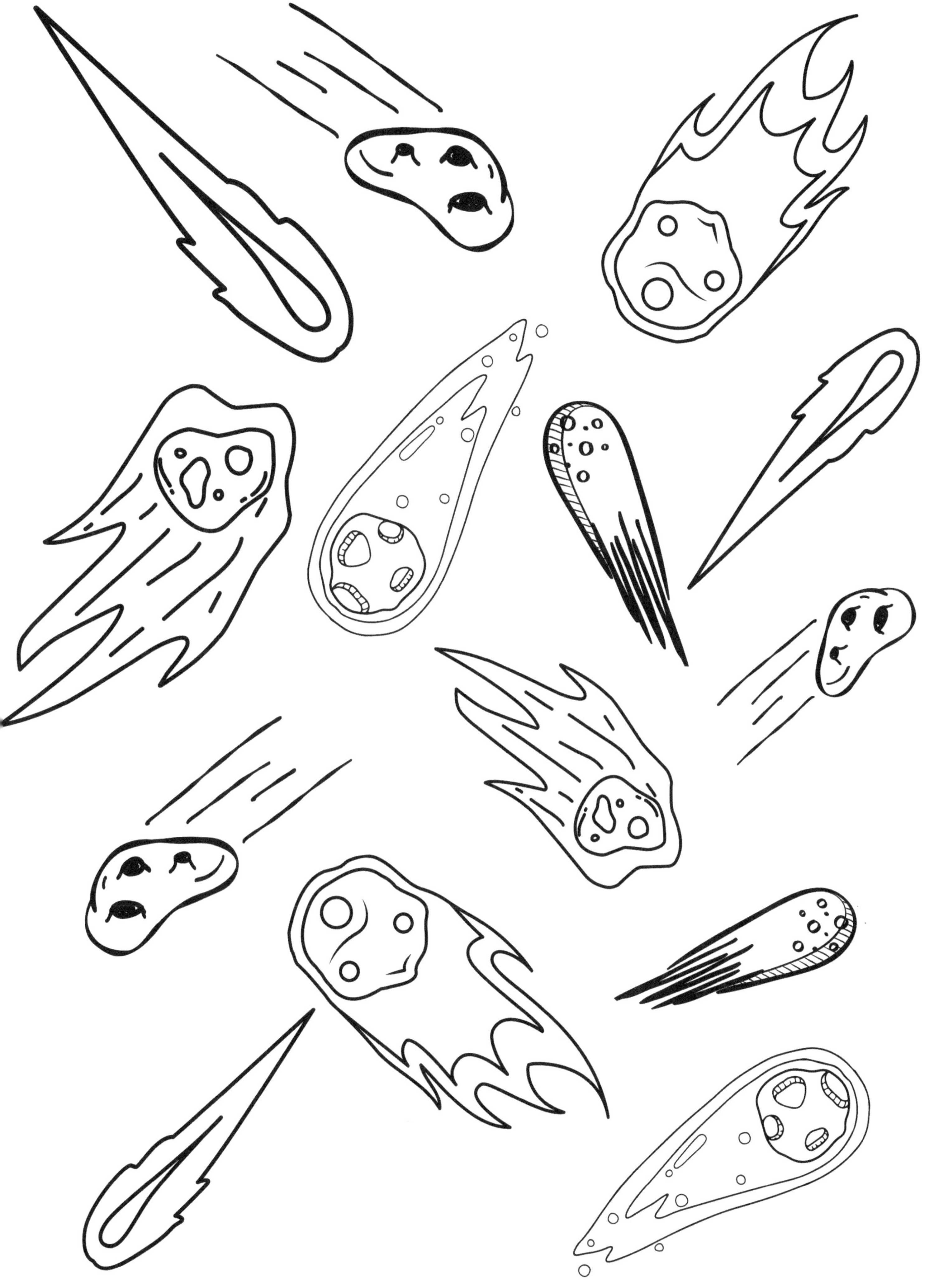

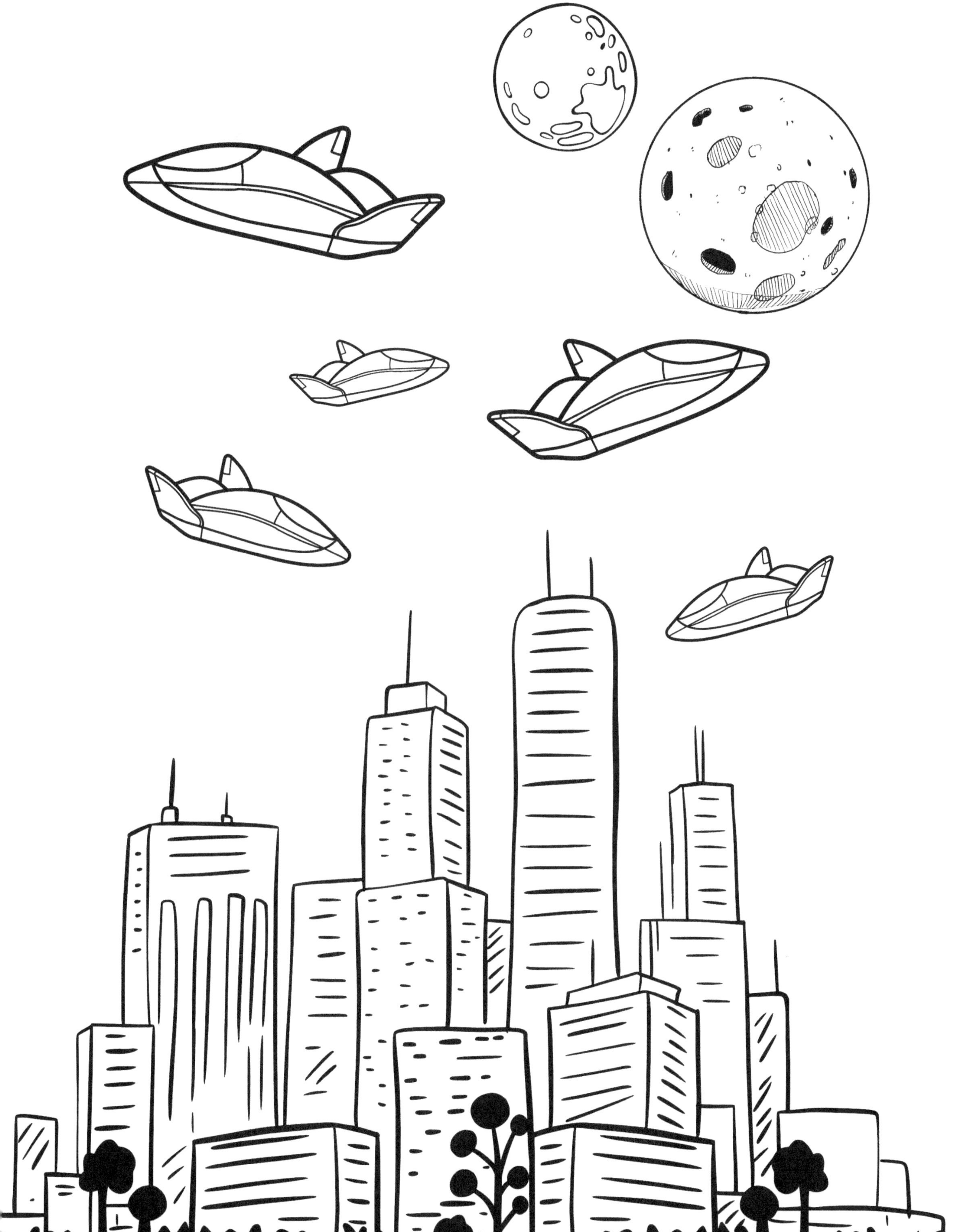

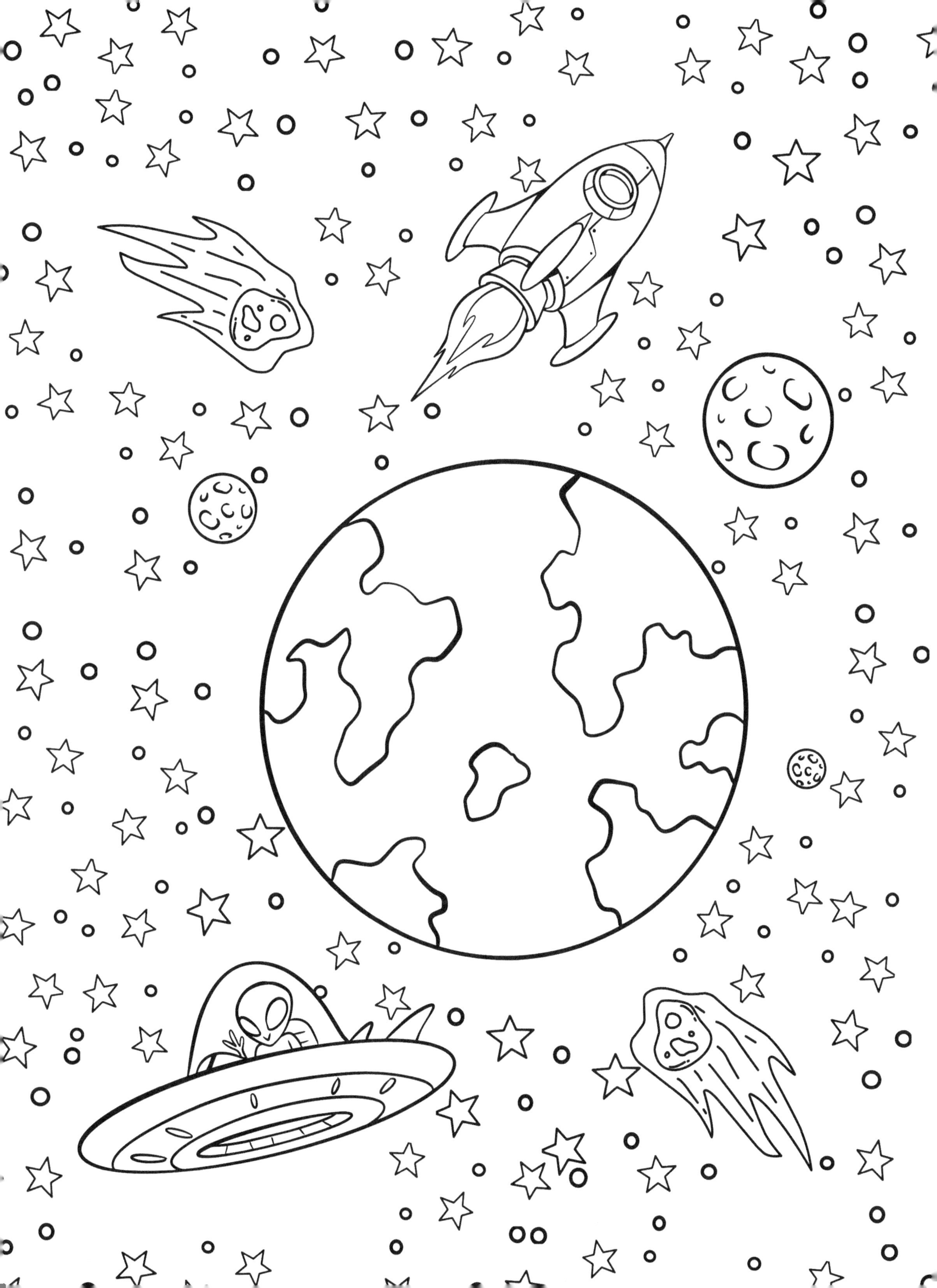

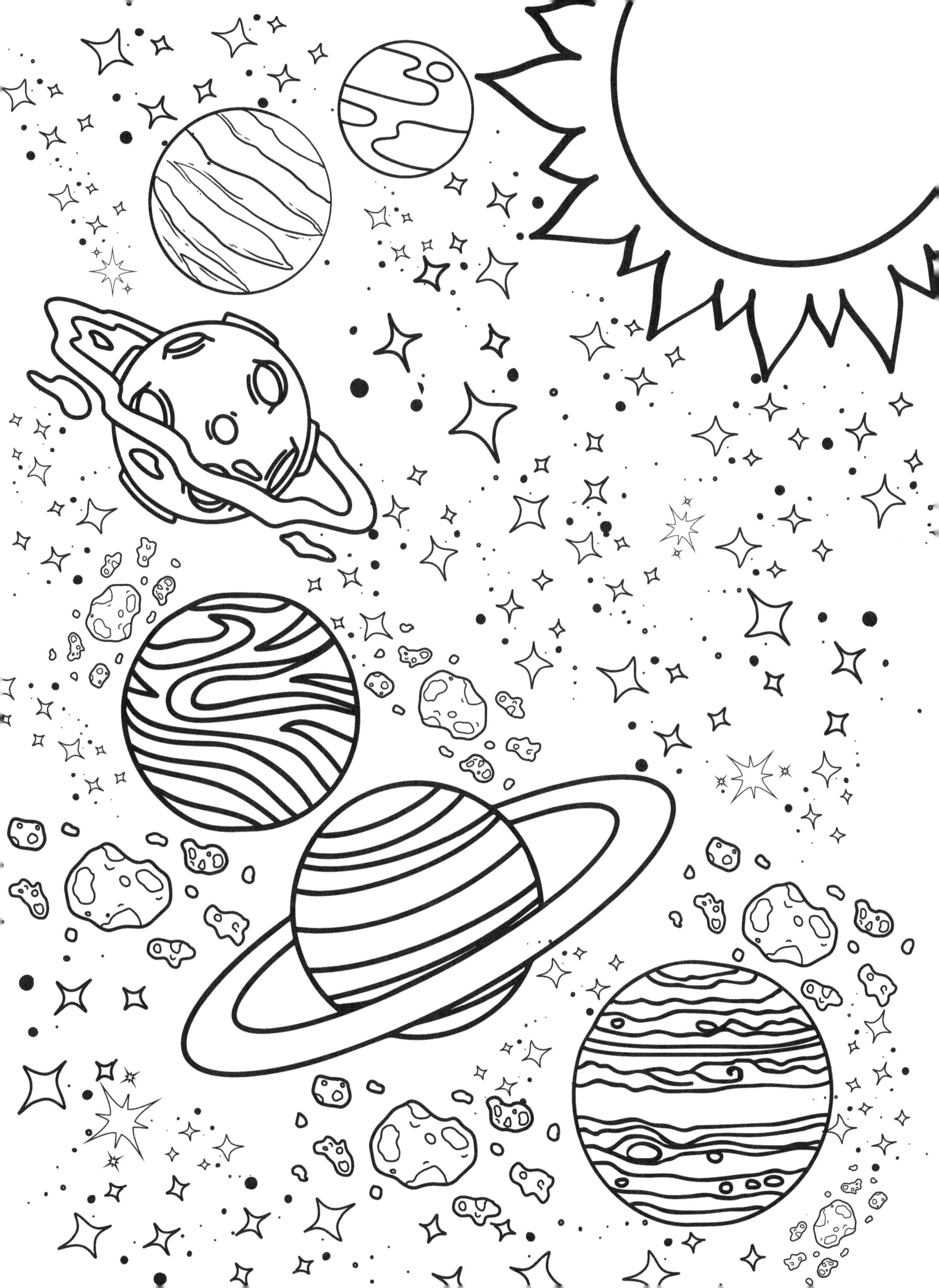

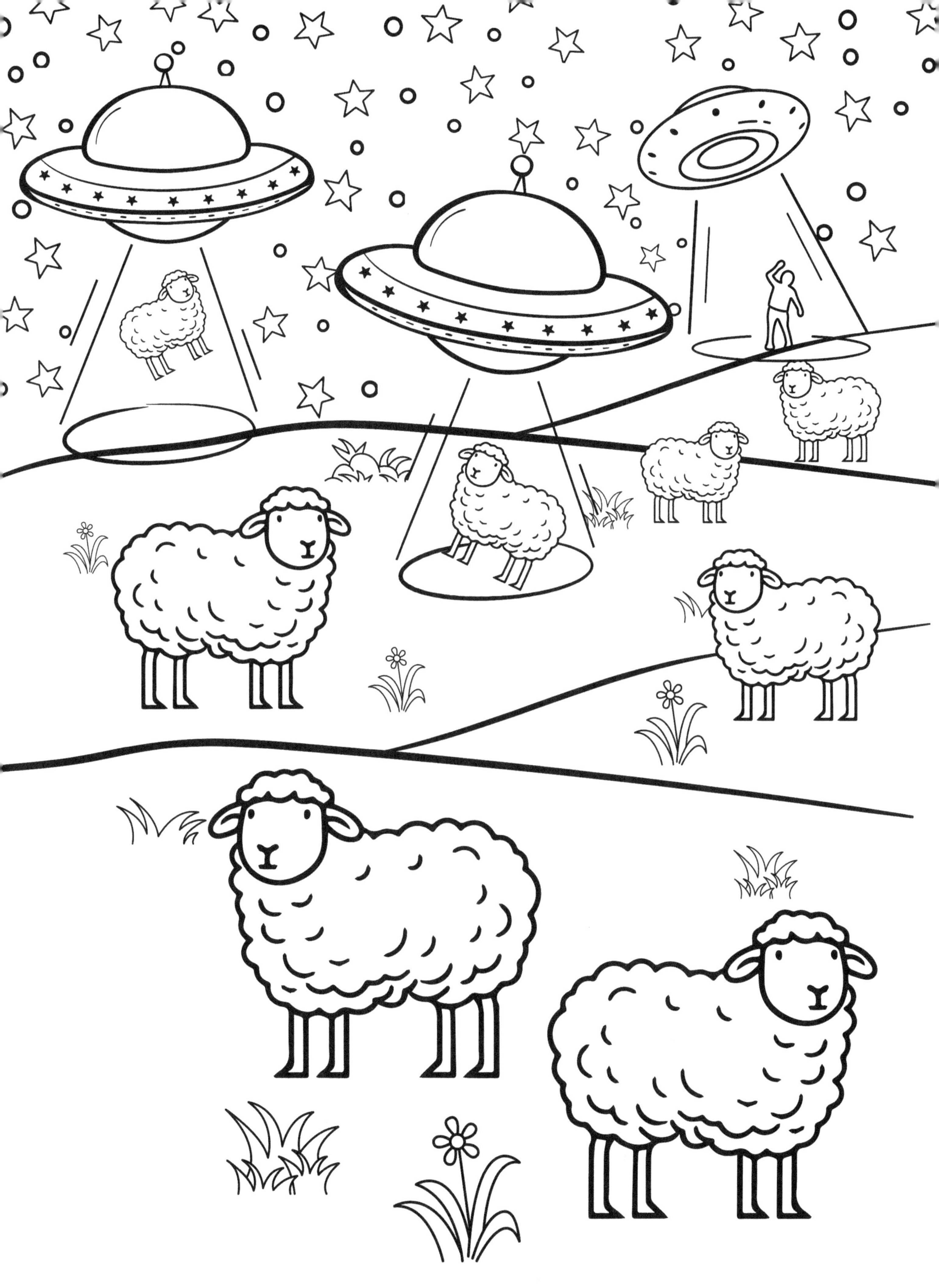

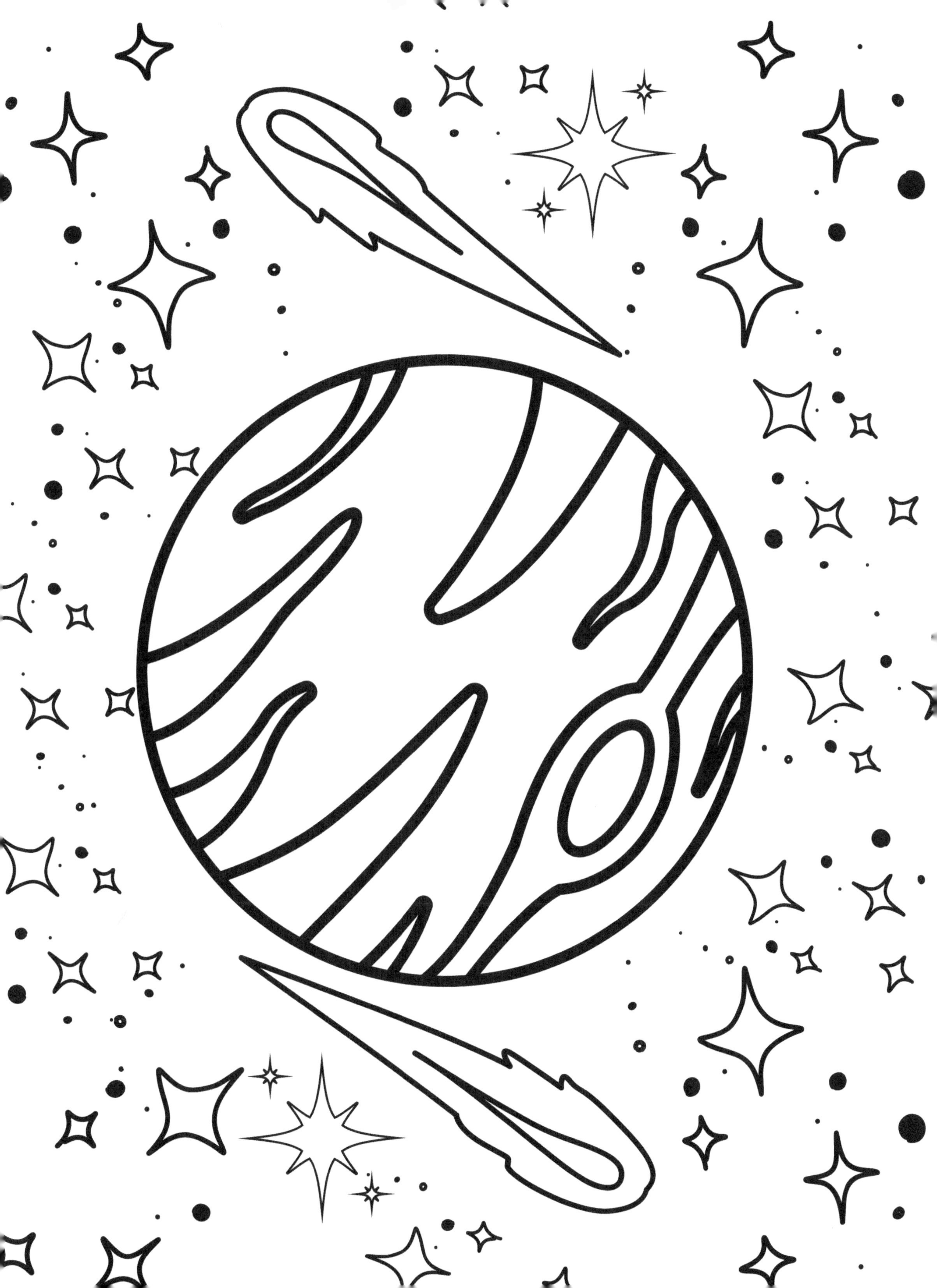

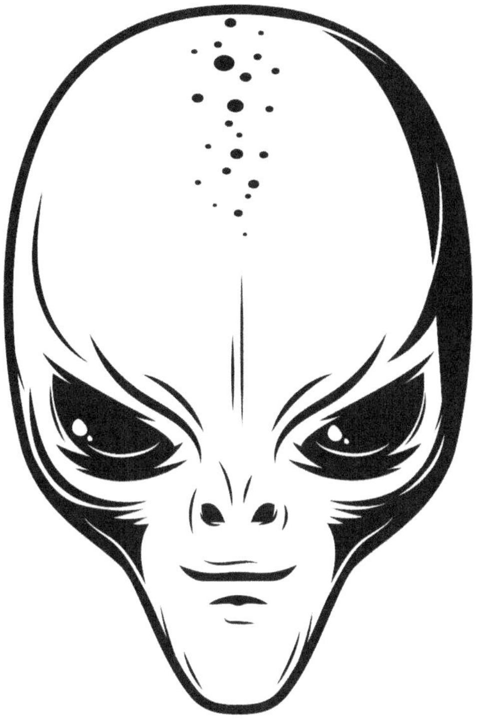
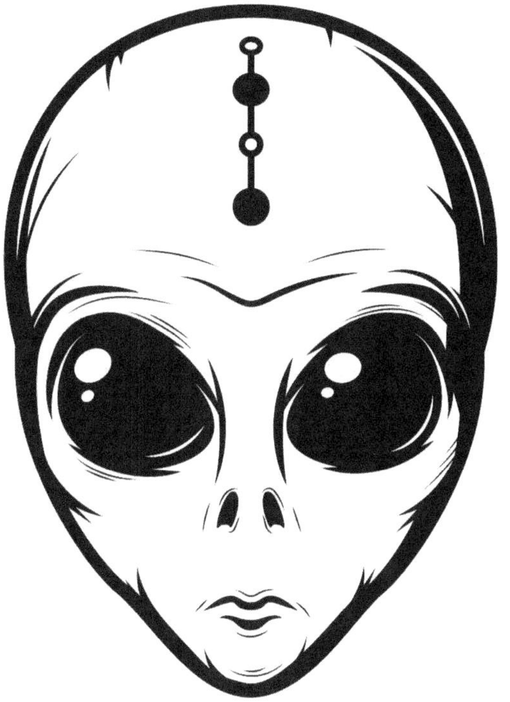
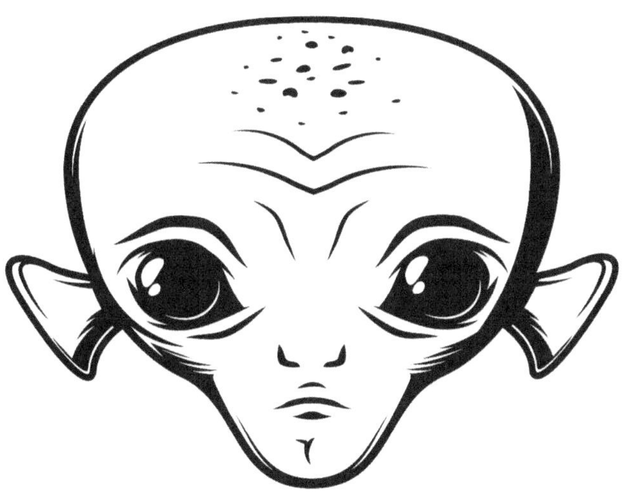
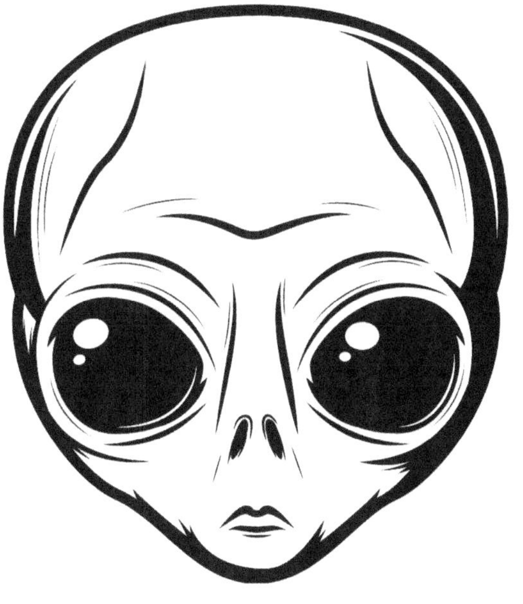
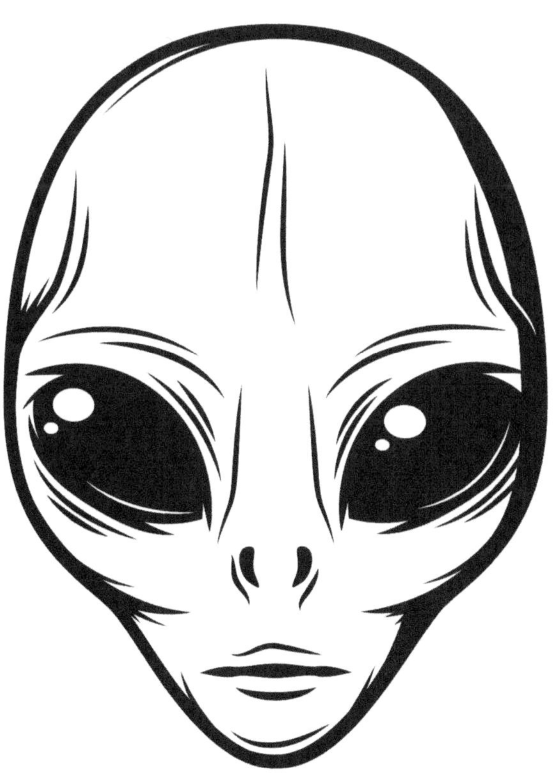
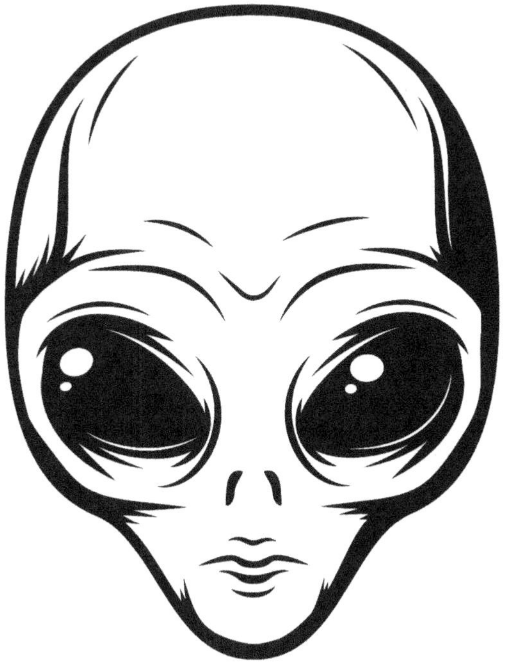

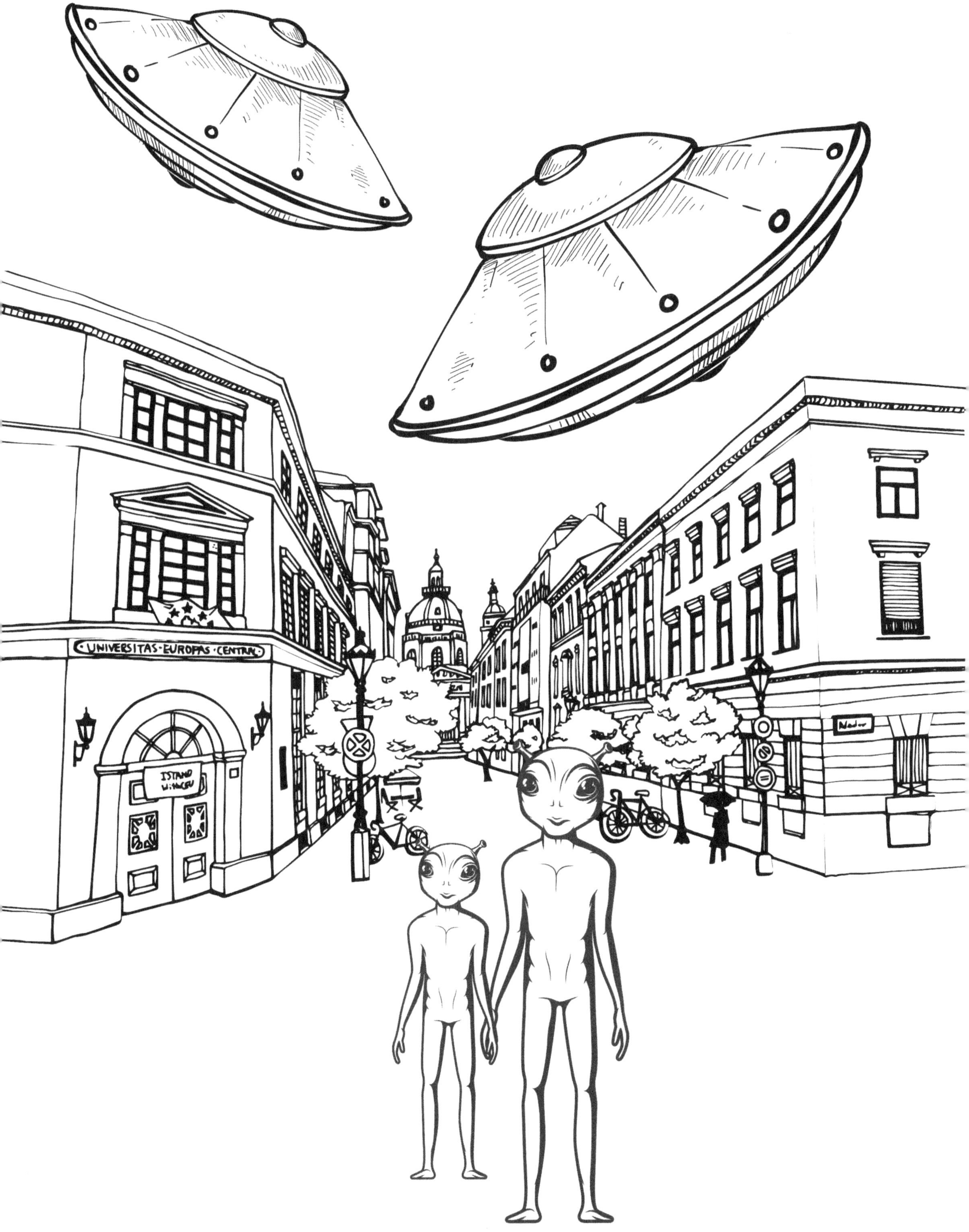
·UNIVERSITAS·EUROPAS·CENTRAL·
ISTAND

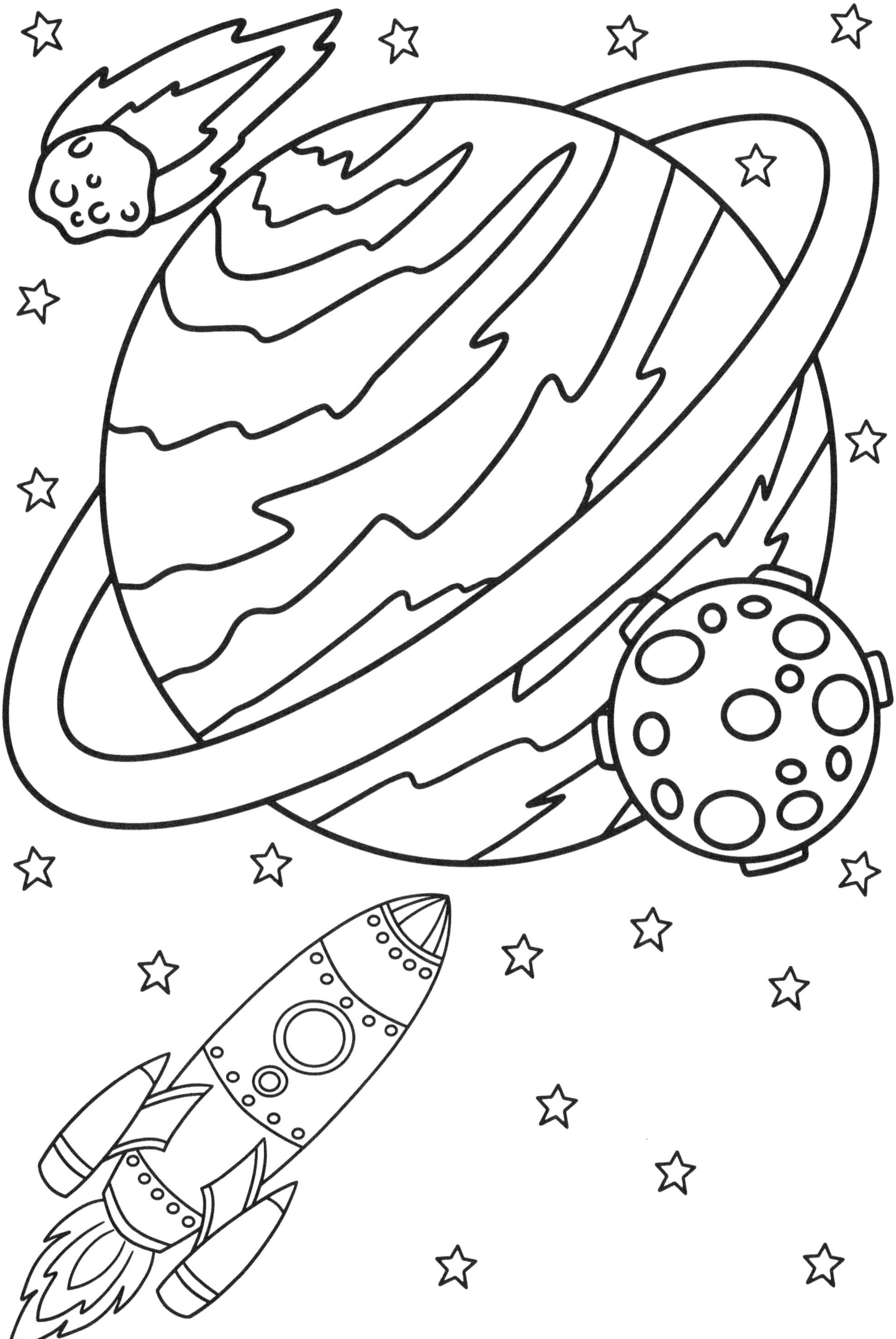

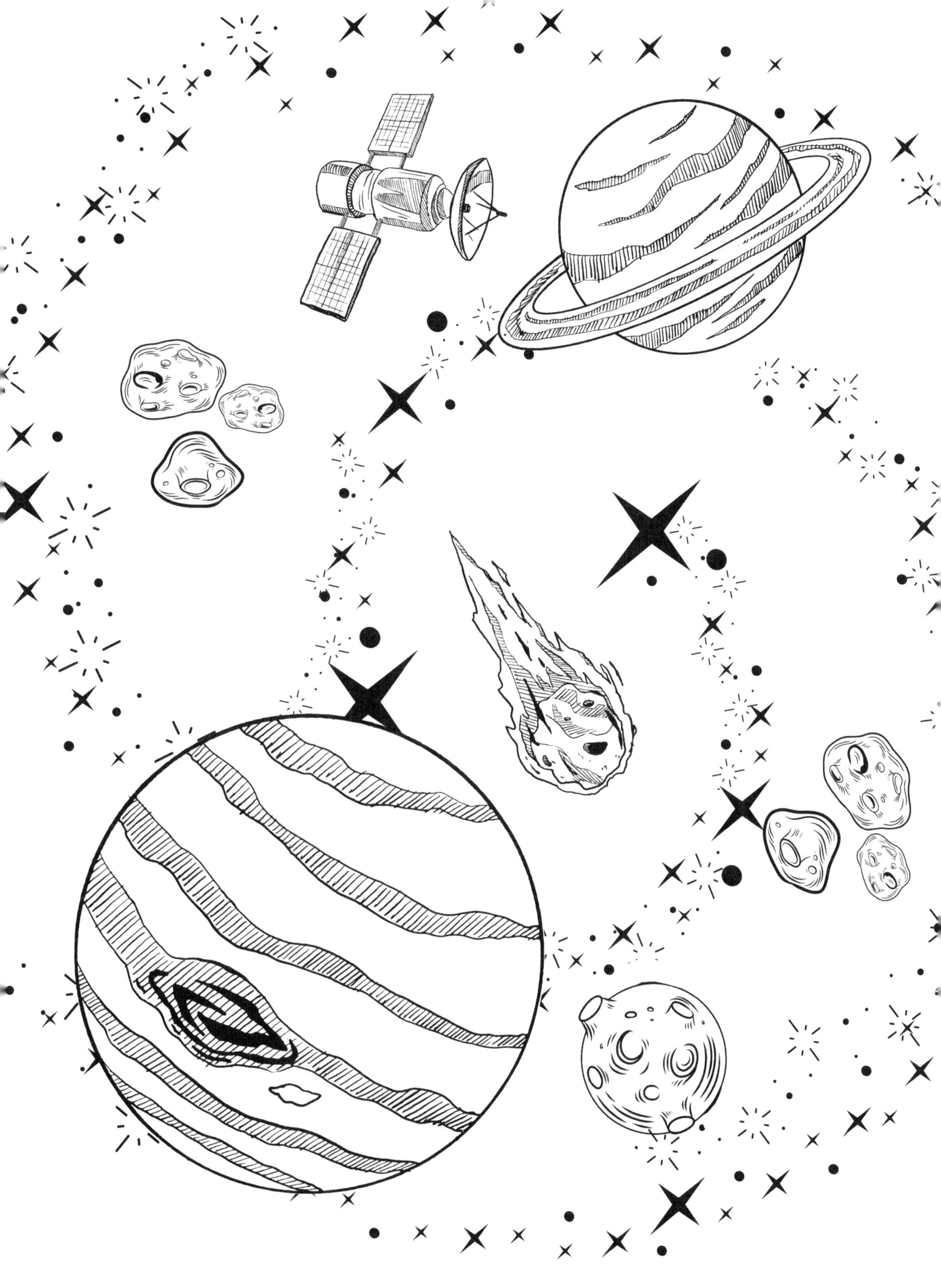

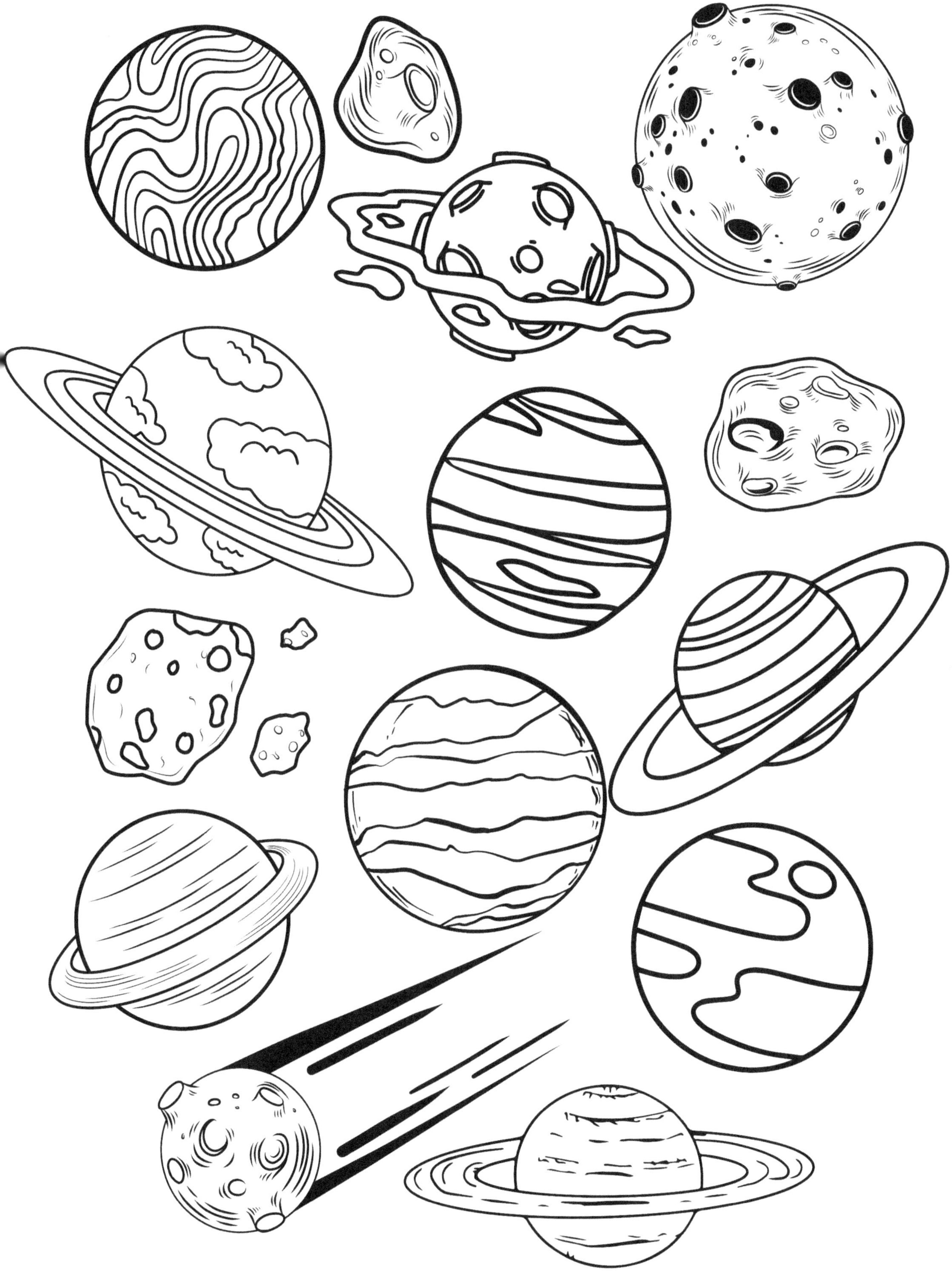

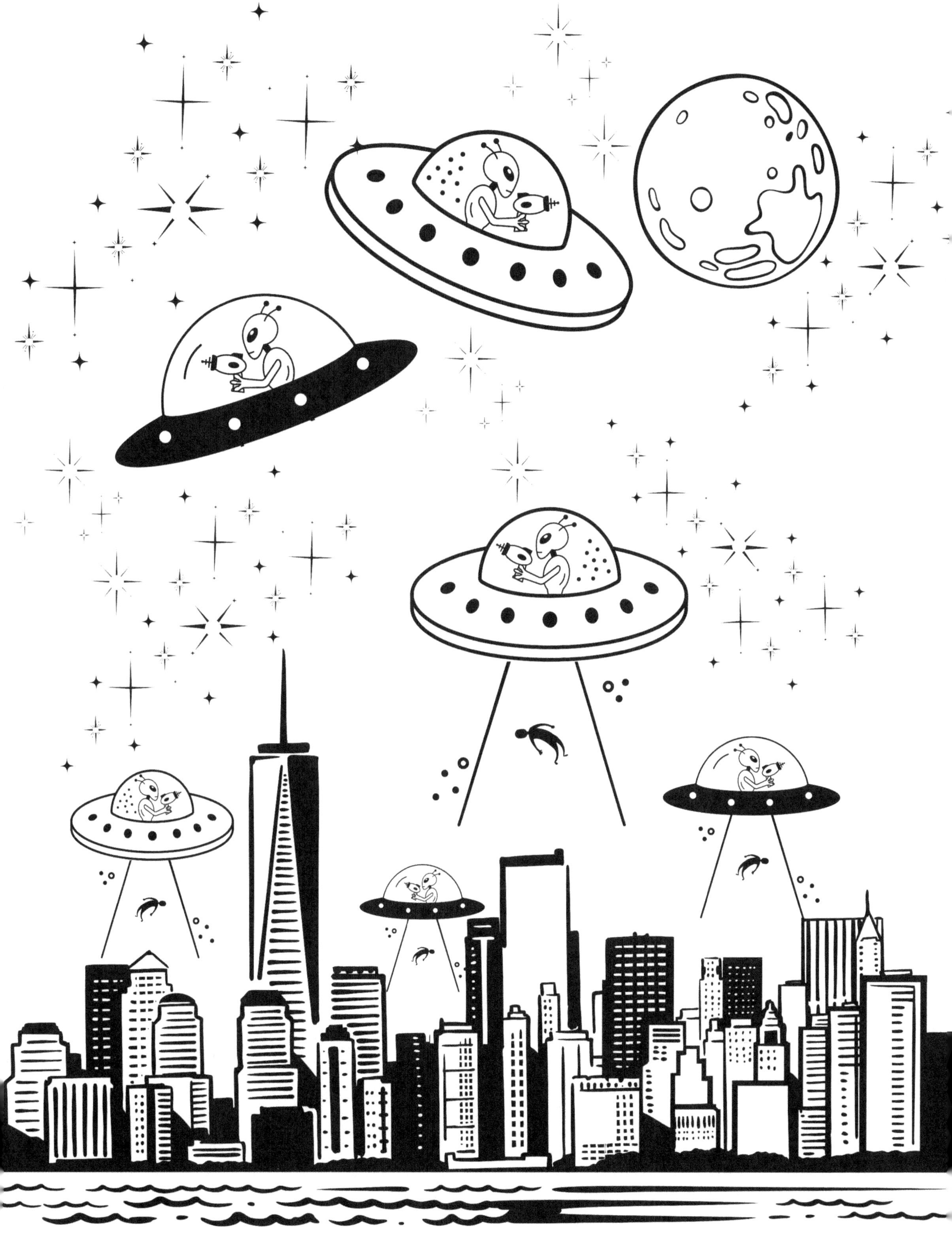

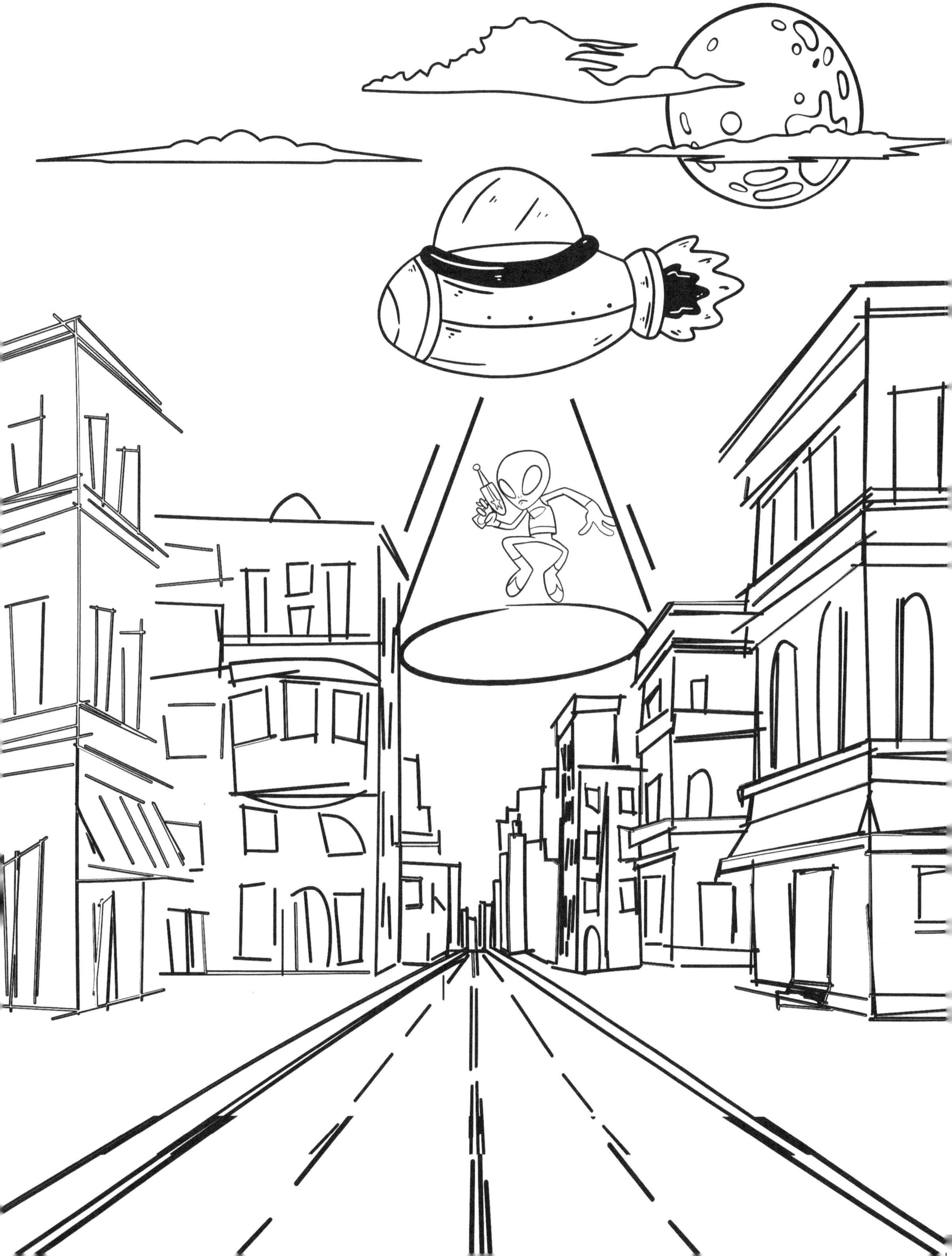

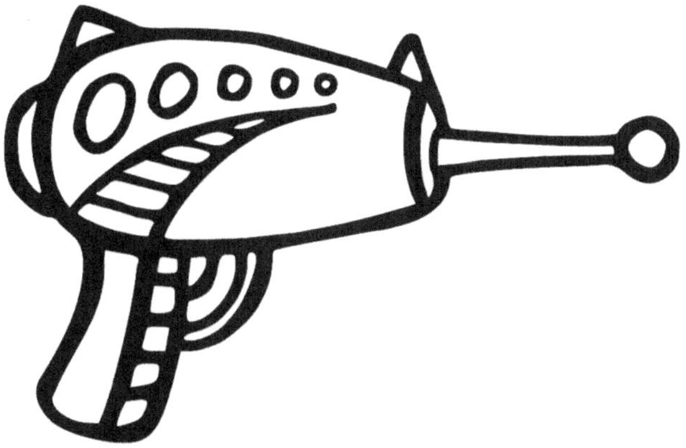
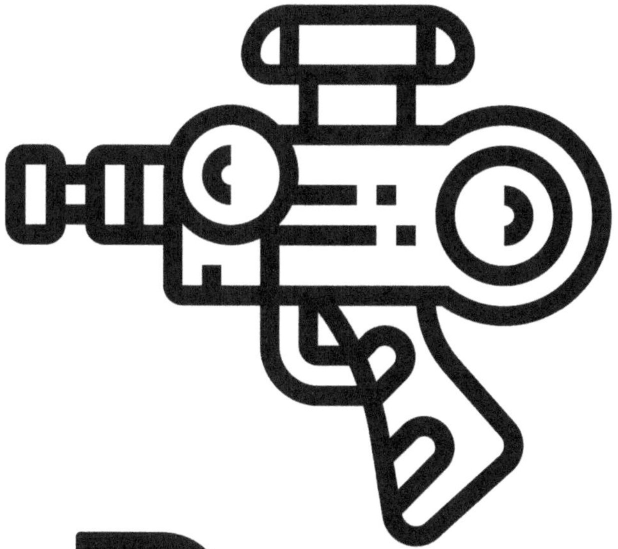
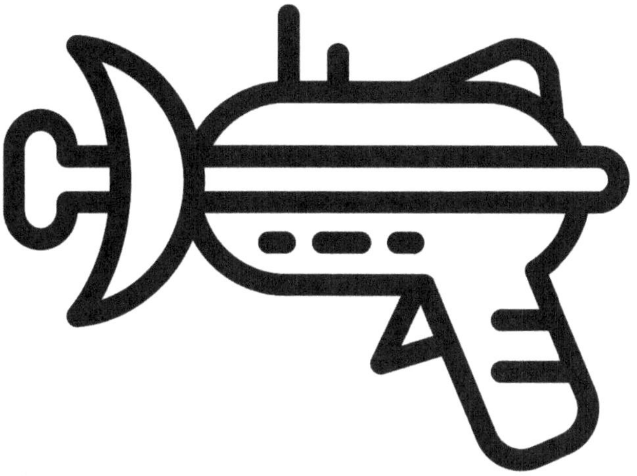
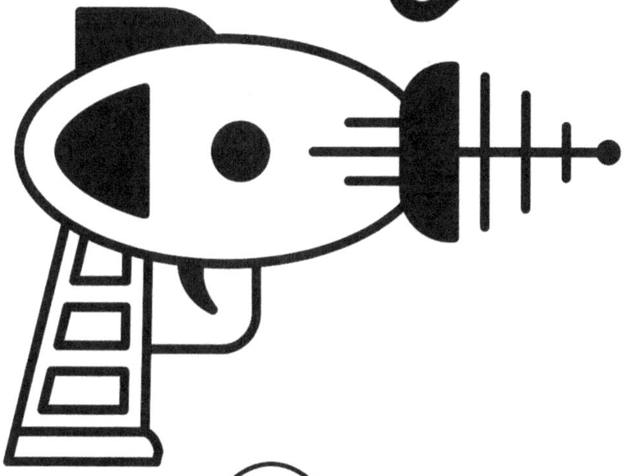
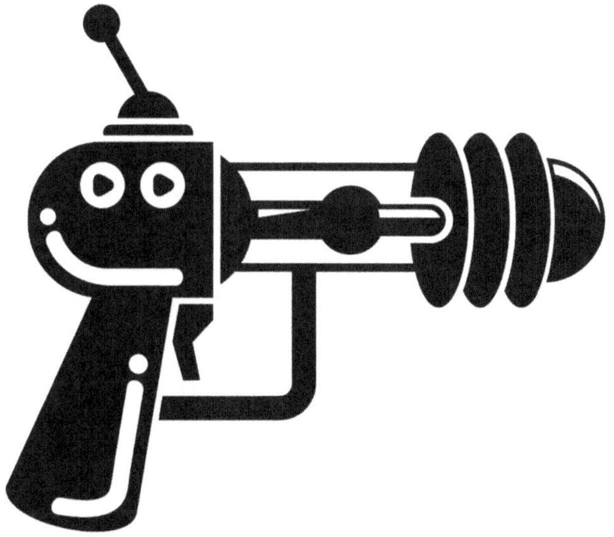
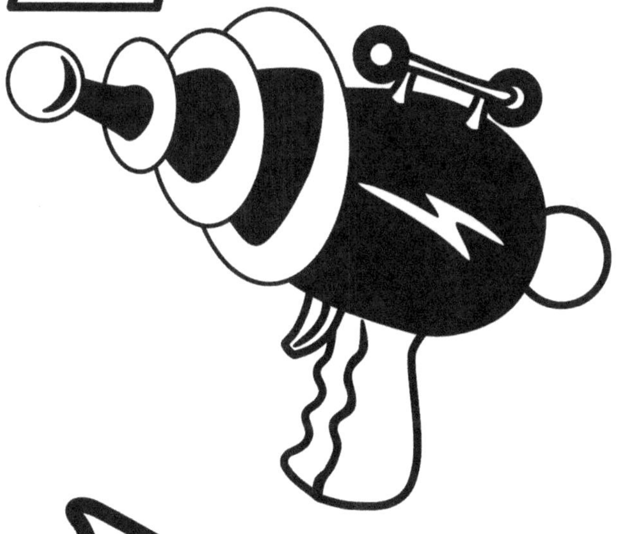
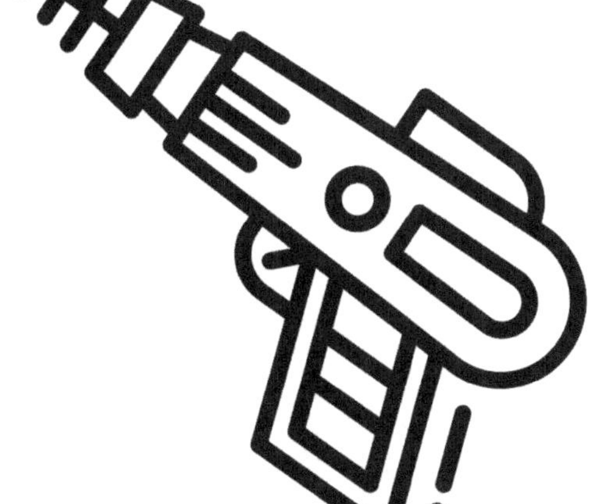
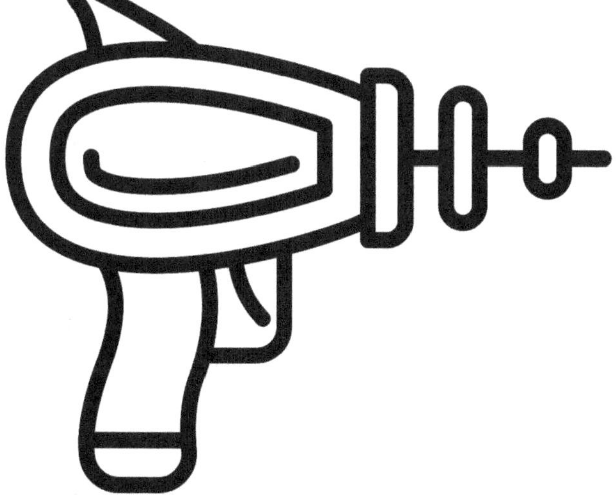

www.ingramcontent.com/pod-product-compliance
Lightning Source LLC
Chambersburg PA
CBHW062118220526
45471CB00010B/3785
9798321072127